Grassroots Ecumenicity

Grassroots Ecumenicity

Case Studies in Local Church Consolidation

Horace S. Sills, Editor

UNITED CHURCH PRESS
PHILADELPHIA   BOSTON

The scripture quotations in this publication are (unless otherwise indicated) from the *Revised Standard Version of the Bible,* copyrighted 1946 and 1952 by the Division of Christian Education, National Council of Churches, and are used by permission.

Library of Congress Catalog Card Number 66–23993

Preface

THE SUCCESS of the ecumenical movement depends on faith and trust, with a willingness on the part of everyone concerned to emphasize these qualities more than the individual differences of the local churches. There must be a channel through which the Spirit of God can move freely to do his will. The men and women of the local congregations involved in the ecumenical consolidations recorded in this book provided such a channel and exercised abundant faith and trust to achieve their desired goal. The uniting of their local congregations is a testimony to God's power and love. My gratitude and heartfelt thanks go to these local people for the contributions that they have made to the church in a new age.

None of these consolidations could have been achieved were it not for committed pastors who could see beyond tomorrow, concerned denominational executives who were willing to give-and-take while laboring in love for the whole church, and councils of churches through which the denominations have learned to share in the total mission of the church. The deeds of such men are recorded in the case studies in this book. As they move on to other communities to face the problems of the church there, they will have an increased knowledge and love of the church because they have seen what congregations can do when there is sufficient concern about the mission of the local church. My sincere gratitude is hereby expressed to these key people. It is not possible to name all of those who participated in these negotiations; however, a list will be provided on request by the editor.

I am especially indebted to my colleagues on the staff of the Department of the Church in Town and Country of the United Church of Christ and to our national committee both for their support in all the phases of our work and for first suggesting that this information be brought together in book form. I am also obligated to my colleagues in other denominations whose assistance in obtaining information on these consolidations was invaluable. My special thanks go to Dr. Martin L. Tozer, director of missions and parish development, Central Pennsylvania Synod of the Lutheran Church in America, for the lessons in interchurch cooperation he has taught me in the years of our association.

HORACE S. SILLS

Lancaster, Pennsylvania

Contents

Chapter One

✠

Growth at the Grassroots

A FEW YEARS AGO the world in which man lived was large in comparison with his exploratory capabilities. Through the advancement of technical science and industry this world has become increasingly small, so that no country and no people are more than a few hours distance from any other country or people. But even as the achievements of man bring him closer to his neighbors in terms of travel and communications, his ideologies often prevent him from exercising neighborliness. The world, though small and accessible, is fragmented and divided.

The church seeks to perform its mission in such a world. This mission is to heal and to reconcile. Although the church is essentially one, as the world is one, its unity and purpose in mission is obscured by the outward appearances of its own fragmentations. For the church to be able to fulfill its purpose of existence, and thus its mission, it must plainly demonstrate, through its being, its own willingness to be reconciled and united.

The record of the church in the twentieth century is one of encouraging achievements toward such unity. Between 1925 and 1964 nearly forty church unions of national and world significance were accomplished. In some instances the uniting groups were of different denominational backgrounds as were the formulations of the United Church of Canada, the Church of South India, and the United Church of Christ. In keeping with the ecumenical spirit of this day consultations are continuing among church leaders in the hope of bringing about even greater unity. The United Presbyterian Church in the

United States of America, the Protestant Episcopal Church, the United Church of Christ, the Methodist Church, the Evangelical United Brethren, and the Disciples of Christ—with a combined membership of over twenty-one million members—have been involved in conversations for more than four years on the question of church union. The Second Vatican Council with its ecumenical overtones is still another indication of a movement that brings hope of unity to Christendom.

These hopes and aspirations for church unity will not be realized quickly. It takes time to sift through the heritage of the past and formulate plans for the future. In God's own time the unity will be achieved. But how long can we wait? The changing tide of social circumstance is already affecting the local congregations—especially in town and country communities in America—to such an extent that it becomes imperative that some action be taken. Can unity be achieved on the local level before national groups find ways of accomplishing it? To answer this question one must consider some of the conditions that affect these local groups.

The major thrust of the missionary endeavors of denominational groups in this land was directed primarily toward a rural-oriented constituency. Churches were located at the crossroads of barter and trade, in hamlets of some economic possibilities, and in the open country where farm families could gather easily for worship and fellowship. Large groups of persons were not necessarily the only criterion for the establishment of a particular congregation. Often a congregation was established because of an ethnic heritage or language preference, or because of the means of travel available at that time, or because there was no congregation already established, or because of factions and fractions within a congregation that led some to withdraw and start another congregation of the same denomination in the same community. Whatever the reasons, the early churching of America was thorough.

When one considers the vast changes in agriculture, marketing, transportation, and communication—along with the accompanying shifts in population—the problem of the church in town and country today becomes more understandable. It is estimated that 20 percent of the population moves each year. Many of these people are former farm dwellers who move to the city where greater opportunities are available. In 1900, 40 percent of the population in the United States lived in urban places and 60 percent lived in rural areas. By 1961 the number of urban dwellers had increased to 70 percent of the population. It is further estimated that before very long only 5 to 10 percent of the total population will be employed in agriculture. Add to these facts the knowledge that few isolated communities remain which do not share in the mobility of urban services that has brought the city into the country; one cannot help but recognize that America is rapidly becoming an urbanized society.

The town and country communities have not been oblivious to their changing circumstances. Amid difficulties, to be sure, some have made necessary adjustments. Schools have been reorganized and consolidated. Farm workers are being retrained for other employment. Independent grocers are organizing associations to make wholesale purchases in bulk in order to pass on supermarket savings to their customers. Community leaders are organizing community action groups to plan and develop industrial sites or other projects that will stop the out-migration of people and reverse the tide. With the assistance of state and federal funds and leadership, some town and country communities are in the midst of new development and growth, and the future is one of promise.

There are other areas, however, where this opportunity for future development is not present. The people have already gone. The schools have already been consolidated. The natural resources of these areas and their location are not adequate enough to interest industrial developers to establish new plants in the area. In addition, there is a lack of a sense of community cooperation about them.

Ironically, it is often the church that helps to foster this lack of community. The one institution that in its beginning drew men together in a community relationship is sometimes a dividing agent within the community. People who live together as neighbors, who shop together in the same general store, who belong to the same fire company and the same lodges separate and divide themselves in the multiplicity of their churches. When a difference of opinion concerning a community project or program erupts, it often involves opposition between the members of one congregation and the members of another congregation. The loyalty to a particular church or denomination has prevented more than one community from achieving unity in its social or political life.

The church in town and country is at a crossroads in its history. It must seek better ways of ministering to a dwindling population with a program that is meaningful and that speaks to the needs of its people in the world. It must consider the number of units it supports in a given community as compared with the number of inhabitants to whom it can minister. It must consider its divisions and the unspoken, yet dramatic, adverse message such divisions proclaim to the community. It must justify its existence and its location by the particular message it proclaims and the mission it performs in a given segment of society.

All these musts for the church in town and country have been stated many times before and will be stated many times again before the problems are solved. People are slow to change or even to recognize the necessity for change where the church is concerned. For many, the love of tradition is a more pleasing emotion than the strain of wrestling with the problems of the present age. Prophetic voices in each generation will assuredly call the church to renewal and action.

What action is possible for the church in town and country that is trying to face its future? What adjustments can it make to insure its ministry in areas of declining population? Where does it turn for help and leadership? How will it work out its own salvation? The first requirement in answer to these questions is that the members of the congregation must be willing to approach their problems with open minds. The second requirement is that the congregation must call for assistance from its own denominational leadership.

Denominations have an obligation to their congregations and to society in general to provide the best trained leadership available to assist the congregations in adjustments necessary to meet the needs of the society in which the congregations minister. Men and women with special skills are desperately needed for this task. The denominational executive who maintains only a pastoral relationship with the congregations in his area of responsibility is not able to lead these congregations in responsible planning. He needs other skills. He needs special training in sociology and group dynamics. Above all he needs a sense of mission that enables him to look beyond his own denominational interest and see the total community, recognizing its total needs. This means that he must be cooperatively conversant with leaders of other denominations.

There are many types of adjustment to society's changes that are possible for the local congregations. Many have been tried with varying degrees of success. A wealth of information is available on setting up larger parishes, group ministries, federated churches, community churches, united churches, yoked parishes, and other types of church agreements involving more than one congregation. These have been arranged both denominationally and interdenominationally, and every judicatory executive should be familiar with the mechanics of such adjustment procedures. A request from a local congregation to its denominational executive for assistance should certainly bring from him many helpful suggestions.

It is not possible, nor does it seem necessary, to go into detail here on the variety of church adjustments that are options for congregations faced with a change in their present arrangements. However, since the best known and most often arranged solutions for such congregations have involved those of the same denomination, a cursory look at two types of adjustments will be helpful. The yoked parish and the merger of congregations of the same denomination will be considered.

The Yoked Parish

The denominational approach for church adjustment has been the traditional way of trying to solve the problem of church programming in an area experiencing a decline in population and the accompanying decline in church membership. In areas where a particular denomination has several congregations, it is not usually difficult to have two or more of them plan and work together and/or share the same pastor. Since the beginning of churching in America the yoked parish or pastoral circuit has been an important arrangement for many denominations. It has assured ministerial leadership to even the smallest congregations and has enabled some congregations to continue in existence when some other solution would perhaps have resulted in a better church program for the community. The yoking of churches does not necessarily imply a close harmony between the congregations involved. It may mean that the only thing they have in common is the service of the same pastor. They may plan and promote their own separate programs, contract separately with the pastor for his support, hold and maintain their own property, and in many other ways function as the separate units they are. The yoked relationship enables them to afford the services of the pastor by distributing the cost of his leadership among the participating congregations. The ideal of the yoked parish is to have the congregations join together in much of their program and service to the community.

The advantages of the yoked parish are obvious to congregations faced with this kind of decision about their ministry. The disadvantages are sometimes minimized, since some persons consider it to be more important to continue a congregational tradition than to face a more difficult and drastic type of adjustment. One important disadvantage is the part-time leadership that must necessarily result when a pastor is forced to divide his time and energy among several different congregations in different communities. For one or more of these congregations, the pastor will be a nonresident of the community in which the church is located (except for the rare instance when he serves two congregations in the same community), which adds to the difficulties of an effective ministry. There are other disadvantages, such as the inability of the pastor to participate fully in the Christian education program of each congregation; the multiplicity of meetings and duplication of programs that are necessary and require some pastoral participation; the schedule changes in the worship services which must be effected when three or more congregations are in a yoked arrangement, and which become confusing to members and prospective members; the biweekly worship services, which are sometimes necessary when three or more congregations share the same pastor; and several other disadvantages that affect both pastor and people.

This is not to intimate that all yoked parishes are obsolete or that they are necessarily bad. On the contrary, such an adjustment is sometimes the best arrangement for the congregations involved. The few disadvantages are listed here to indicate that a thorough study should be made of every possibility before unwise decisions that will affect the religious witness of any congregation in any community are made.

Denominational Mergers

The merger of two or more congregations of the same denomination is often the most desirable solution to overchurching. In an area where a particular denomination has more congregational units than the population warrants, the merger of two or more of these units can result in a stronger congregation that would be better able to provide the facilities and program to meet the needs of the people. Such a merger ultimately results in a decline in the competition between the congregations of a given area. It is a strategic withdrawal of at least one of the congregations from an area or community, leaving the resident witness to another group. It results in a better distribution of congregational units for more effective witness and service.

Proper planning at the area or state level and the development of efficient strategy through interdenominational discussions is essential even when congregations of the same denomination are merging. Careful planning and the involvement of the local people at every step is absolutely necessary to effect such mergers. It must be understood that when any congregation in a community effects a withdrawal or realignment, or when there is a merger of two congregations, such adjustment will invariably affect the other churches of the area. Denominational executives have the responsibility to share the information of such plans—and to do this before the adjustment is finalized.

Perhaps the greatest disadvantage to denominational mergers of congregations is the necessity of moving at least one of the congregational groups away from its natural community. This happens when two or more congregations in neighboring communities unite and choose either to use one of the existing buildings or to erect another building near the center of the parish area. In either case some of the members must travel out of their home community to attend church in another community. These members, under certain circumstances and in a certain sense, become nonresident members of the church they attend. Their exodus from their natural community to attend worship on Sunday morning further separates them from the rest of the churches of their community.

It is questionable whether denominations, congregations, or communities can any longer afford the luxury of purely denominational adjustments of congregations. The pluralism, secularization, and urbanization of society demands that denominations think and act differently about their congregations than most have been wont to do. The religious institution has been the slowest of all social institutions to face its responsibilities to society. The resistance to change within the religious institution may be a natural attempt of people to keep a place in their lives free and uncontaminated by what they believe is happening in the rest of society. While trying nobly to hold onto the past through the church, however, they prevent the church from becoming the relevant force that the changing society needs.

Interdenominational Consolidation

In the past few years some congregations in local communities, with the help and blessing of judicatories and local and state councils of churches, have been able to unite across denominational lines. While the denominations continue their own consultations, these congregations are actually achieving organic union and thereby improving their witness and assuring their future.

The process whereby interdenominational consolidation is achieved is usually for one or more of the congregations involved to dissolve (disband) for the purpose of permitting the members to unite with the congregation of the denomination that will remain. The result is a stronger congregational group with a united program and witness. By having one denominational affiliation, cumbersome organizational problems sometimes encountered in other types of interdenominational cooperative ministries are eliminated.

The negotiation procedures used to achieve consolidation of congregations in a few such communities have been recorded in this book from information furnished by the people of the churches involved. The step-by-step procedure is presented here for the information of judicatories, councils of churches, and local church members who may be interested in this approach to the problems of the church on the local level. For the most part, no guidelines were available to the congregations in their attempts at consolidation. These congregations felt a need for change and unity and arrived at their decision after many discussions and agreements.

There has been little attempt to evaluate these case studies. They are presented on their own merits, and the negotiation procedures used speak for themselves. Suffice it to say that for the congregations involved in these discussions, the process as recorded here was successful. Unity was achieved, competition was eliminated, strength was gained, and a spirit of community in areas other than the church was realized.

A word needs to be said on the beginning of such discussions in a community. Those to whom a consolidation will mean the most are the members of the local congregations. Sometimes the local people may feel that consolidation is the best answer to their local church problems. They may even begin to discuss consolidation locally on an informal basis, only to discover that their talks have led them to preconceived ideas that cannot be realized. This often leads to disappointment and even to greater separation of the congregations if not handled properly. Because of the various governmental practices of the denominations that might become involved in local discussions of this type, it is always the best practice for the local group to *invite the denominational executives to discuss the question of consolidation even before informal decisions have been made.*

Through local and state councils of churches, the denominational executives who are responsible for church adjustment have discovered ways of working in harmony with one another. They have realized that more can be achieved through cooperative endeavors than through a unilateral approach. Many state councils of churches are now asking their member denominations to consider the adjustments in town and country areas as seriously as they are considering the location of new churches in new communities. Some councils are engaged in important studies of their churches in town and country areas, which will reveal more accurately what kinds of adjustment are necessary to bring about more efficient church units. These studies are shared with all participating denominational groups, and planning for the future of some communities on this basis becomes an interdenominational project.

Any community interested in exploratory discussions on interdenominational consolidation of congregations should keep in mind a few basic factors.

1. The goal of the congregations should be to create a more efficient and effective ministry in the name of the Lord rather than be motivated to this adjustment from a purely economic concern.

2. The judicatory should know about and approve the discussions. Judicatory executives should participate in the discussions if possible.

3. The local pastors should be committed to the idea and need for consolidation and, if possible, continue to serve the congregations until a decision has been reached.

4. To determine the denomination to which the consolidated congregation will be affiliated is probably the most difficult decision to be reached. Each person should maintain an open mind until this question is ready to be answered by the total membership of each congregation in the discussion.

It is too early in the history of these known consolidated congregations to evaluate the lasting impact they are making in the communities they serve. Initial observations are extremely encouraging, however. A second series of case studies of the congregations in these seven communities will be made later. The results of these studies, showing the effectiveness of the mission and the lasting qualities of the endeavors, will offer even more help to communities that are interested in this kind of adjustment.

Interdenominational consolidation of congregations in local communities may not be the final word in adjustments necessary to help the church be the church in every community. It appears at this stage, however, that for some communities it is the best answer that can be proposed.

No denominational group alone will be able to solve the problems faced by the church in town and country. If the problem of overchurching and under-pastoring is to be corrected, it will have to be approached in the spirit of cooperation by those denominations affected. The local church in many town and country communities cannot afford to wait until the denominational consultation on church union has been brought to fruition. The case studies recorded here will indicate to those who are interested that answers can be found when all who are concerned will search for them.

Chapter Two

✠

Schellsburg United Church of Christ Schellsburg, Pennsylvania

CONTINUING EDUCATION opportunities for pastors serving town and country parishes provide essential information and instruction for those who seek to keep abreast of the rapidly changing characteristics of the American scene. Land-grant colleges, through their extension departments and continuing-education programs, are well-equipped to offer many of these opportunities. The Michigan State University at East Lansing, Michigan, has been a pioneer institution in the development of a two-week training program designed especially for town and country pastors. The interdenominational and interfaith aspects of the school provide the atmosphere for creative thought and expression on the church and its mission.

In the summer of 1960, one of the elective courses at Michigan State was entitled "The Rural Church in a Changing Society." The instructor provided a case study and an analysis of the procedure followed in uniting five congregations of the same denomination in a small community in Pennsylvania. The students, many of whom were serving in overchurched communities themselves, were much impressed. The then pastor of the United Church of Christ congregation in Schellsburg, Pennsylvania, and his wife, who were enrolled in this course, raised some serious questions regarding the church situation in Schellsburg. Time was given in the class situation for a description of these conditions.

The community of Schellsburg for a number of years had been experiencing a decline in population to the present number of 288 persons. Schellsburg was once a fairly prosperous agricultural area, with dairy farming as the prime source of income. Even this industry began to wane because of sharp competition with the Ohio dairy market and the market of other eastern Pennsylvania counties. When the state began to purchase land for a park in the area, many farmers were eager to sell. The present residents of Schellsburg receive much of their income from the state park visitors.

The pastor reported to the class that four congregations had tried desperately to maintain their particular witness in the community for many years, even though handicapped by a declining population and low income. Membership in these congregations were: United Church of Christ (UCC) 82; Methodist 79; Presbyterian 55; and Lutheran 68. The Methodist building burned some years earlier and the congregation rented the Presbyterian building in which to hold its worship services on alternate Sundays. The Lutheran and UCC congregations had church buildings in the same block, while the Lutheran congregation also owned a house which once had been used as a parsonage, but which in later years had been rented and allowed to deteriorate.

Each congregation shared a ministry with from two to five other congregations. No minister had resided in the community in several years. Each congregation conducted services every other week. The Presbyterian, Methodist, and UCC congregations sponsored a union church school, which met each week. The Lutheran congregation had no church school.

The situation as described by the pastor was obviously a problem of overchurching. His colleagues in the course discussed ways of strengthening the Christian witness in Schellsburg and encouraged the pastor to seek the assistance of his fellow pastors in the community and the state council of churches in beginning discussions with the local people to consider various alternatives for a better ministry.

The State Council of Churches Shows Concern

In the fall of 1960, arising out of the same class discussions at Michigan State University, preliminary discussions took place through the Town and Country Division of the Pennsylvania Council of Churches between representatives of the respective denominations regarding the feasibility of a common project at Schellsburg. The project was referred to the Pennsylvania Council of Churches' Division of Missions (successor agency to the Town and Country Division) for further consideration. Representatives of the four denominations having a congregation in the community agreed that some adjustment should be made among the churches there.

The denominational representatives met with the pastors of the congregations in Schellsburg on January 18, 1961. Each pastor gave a description of the parish he served, noting that it was not possible to give the attention necessary to meet the needs of the Schellsburg community due to demands of the several other congregations in each parish. Again it was the common concern that some adjustment should take place to provide a more effective witness to the community. It was recognized, however, that no adjustment of the churches would be possible unless the members of the congregations took part in the planning. The few members in each congregation had struggled valiantly to maintain their local units amid all the hardships of the past years. The people were concerned about the future, but they were also fearful and somewhat suspicious of those who proposed change. It was essential, therefore, that the denominational representatives meet with the congregations in a joint gathering if the discussions were to proceed.

Through the council of churches and the cooperation of the denominational representatives and pastors of the Schellsburg churches, a joint meeting of the congregations was conducted on April 16, 1961. The social and economic factors of the area were explained, and the alignment of the churches and work load of the pastors were discussed. The members were given the opportunity to ask questions and make suggestions concerning the future of their churches. The denominational representatives were careful to point out that no plan for adjustment had been developed by them; rather, they were hopeful that the members would agree to have their official boards meet together to develop strategy that could later be presented to the congregations for action.

When no response came from the meeting with the congregations by September, 1961, the session of the Presbyterian

church proposed that the Presbyterian church in Schellsburg
be subsidized by the denomination and that a resident pastor
be placed in the community. It was believed that this would
strengthen the Presbyterian congregation and that the other
three congregations would eventually choose to unite with it.
The intentions of this request were completely honorable.
However, such a step would have precluded an adjustment
that could be jointly planned. The Presbyterian synod executive recognized this and agreed to continue to participate in
the local discussions until the people of the community could
decide for themselves what adjustment was necessary.

Involving the Laity

The impetus to evaluate the church situation in Schellsburg
had come from persons outside the community—denominational leaders, state council representatives, and pastors—
rather than from the members themselves. Each congregation
had its own pastor and was able to retain its identity even
though the number attending the services was not large. Since
each congregation had several other churches in its parish
relationship, which contributed to the support of the pastor,
the local expenses were not high. It is understandable, therefore, that the local members felt no sense of urgency to participate in discussions that might lead to a reduction of congregational units in their community.

It was not until March 4, 1962, that representatives of the
official boards of each congregation met with the denominational representatives to plan seriously for the future. The
main accomplishment of this meeting was an agreement to
have each congregation appoint a negotiating committee of
three representatives, plus alternates, to work out a plan of
adjustment. A committee of twelve persons would be able to
establish relationships for a freer exchange of ideas than a
large group made up of all the official board members. The
negotiating committee would have no authority to commit the
congregations to any adjustment, but would have authority to
make recommendations. Any recommendations that would
come from the committee would be presented to the official
boards of the congregations for approval before the congregations would be asked to consider them.

When the negotiating committee met on May 20, 1962, the
idea of making some change in the church situation in the

community gained momentum. Discussions centered around the possibility of having the four congregations consolidate into one unit. A straw vote of the committee members indicated that there was enough interest in this possibility to ask the congregations to consider it.

Plans were made to have the four congregations meet separately and discuss church consolidation in Schellsburg. The committee thought it would be possible to ask the congregations to take a straw vote on consolidation; they even believed that a plan could be developed which would reveal a denominational preference.

The committee agreed to suggest to the congregations that a consolidation take place. Each church member would be given a ballot on which he could mark his denominational preference. It was assumed that each member would have as his first choice the denomination of which he was already a member. He would be asked, therefore, to mark his second and third denominational preference.

The strategy behind this plan was simple. If a majority of members named the same denomination as a second choice, there would be little or no difficulty in achieving consolidation and deciding on denominational affiliation at the same time.

A Wrong Guess

Even the best plans and intentions are not always fulfilled. Such was the case when the four congregations met and acted on the recommendation of the negotiating committee. When the ballots from the straw votes were tabulated on July 15, 1962, it was clear that the members were not as prepared to make changes as some had hoped. The results of this vote were as follows:

Congregation	Members on Roll	Preferential Denominational Vote					Total Votes
		L	M	UCC	P	Abstaining	
Lutheran	68	0	8	5	3	2	18
Presbyterian	55	0	9	3	0	6	18
Methodist	79	2	0	4	6	2	14
UCC	82	18	18	0	3	2	41

The decision of the negotiating committee that resulted in the straw vote of the congregations was premature. Not enough time was taken to let the people become accustomed to the idea of consolidation. The straw vote indicated that the people were not convinced that this was the best way of solving their problems.

When the denominational representatives met to review the action of the congregations, the question was raised regarding the possibility of having these representatives suggest the denominational affiliation of a consolidated congregation in Schellsburg. The circumstances in the community appeared to be such that each congregation would insist on retaining its own identity. Would they accept a consolidation and would they accept a recommendation on affiliation made as a joint proposal of the denominational representatives? The negotiating committee agreed that this approach would be more acceptable to the members.

It was not until September 22, 1962, that the denominational representatives were able to meet to decide on their recommendation. After reviewing all the factors involved—the parish alignments, the location of other denominational congregations in the area, the size of the congregations, and conditions of the buildings—the representatives agreed that church consolidation was the answer to the Schellsburg situation and that the resultant congregation should be affiliated with the United Church of Christ.

When this recommendation was reported to the negotiating committee on October 28, 1962, there was general agreement that it should be presented to the congregations for action even though not every member of the committee personally approved the recommendation. A period of six weeks would elapse before the congregations would be asked to vote. During this time each denominational representative would meet with his congregation to lead them in a discussion of the matter. Everyone hoped that during this period the members would be able to recognize that the community could support one church better than four, and that the total religious witness could be improved if a consolidation would take place. The recommendation on denominational affiliation would also be explained. This recommendation was based on the size and condition of the UCC building, the size of the UCC congregation, and the general location of other churches in the area.

The congregations met on December 2, 1962, to vote on the recommendation that there be a consolidation of the four congregations into one congregation that would be affiliated with the United Church of Christ. The ballots were opened on December 9, 1962. The following votes were tabulated:

Congregation	Yes	No	Abstaining	Total Votes
Lutheran	10	14	0	24
Methodist	8	12	0	20
Presbyterian	0	29	3	32
UCC	26	9	1	36

The recommendation had been rejected. The congregations had chosen to keep things as they were.

A New Proposal

The decision of the congregations not to consolidate would lead to a sure dissolution of more than one of them in a few short years. Although the least number of members recorded in any of the congregations was 55, this did not mean that all were supporting members. A later review of the congregational rolls showed that some members of the congregations in Schellsburg had not lived in the community for many years. Some had even united with other congregations, but their names had not been removed from the church record. Attendance in all the congregations was much lower than the membership figures would indicate. At times there would be only 12 or 15 attending worship services.

These facts were discussed by the denominational representatives when they met on March 28, 1963, to determine if negotiations for adjustment of the churches should continue. It was decided that something should be done before the condition deteriorated further. A consolidated congregation still seemed the best answer and there appeared to be no real reason to change the recommendation that it be affiliated with the United Church of Christ. How this idea could be presented again to the congregations was the problem.

A plan was developed for congregational consideration. It was proposed that the United Church of Christ denomination appoint a new pastor who would serve all the congregations in the community. Each pastor serving in Schellsburg would be asked not to perform any ministerial functions there, but to devote full time to the other congregations of his parish. The UCC pastor would be officially recognized as the regular sup-

ply pastor of the Presbyterian, Methodist, and Lutheran congregations and would provide services for these congregations
in their own buildings. The plan was to be presented to the
congregations on a two-year experimental basis, at the end of
which a revote on consolidation and affiliation with the UCC
denomination would be taken.

This proposal was discussed with the pastors serving the
Schellsburg churches in the afternoon of May 23, 1963. Each
pastor agreed to the plan if adopted by the congregations. The
appointed pastor, they agreed, should be a graduate of both
college and seminary and have several years experience in the
parish ministry.

At the congregational meetings called for the evening of
May 23, 1963, the proposal regarding pastoral arrangements
was made to the members. A vote was taken in each congregation on its willingness to participate in the experiment, and
each one voted in the affirmative. In fact, there were many
who expressed the belief that this should have been the first
proposal made to them.

Moving Toward Unity

It had been agreed that the pastors would continue to serve
the churches in Schellsburg until the UCC denomination
could locate the right pastor to serve the total community.
These pastors provided the leadership necessary to bring the
four congregations together for joint worship services during
the summer of 1963. The first joint service was conducted on
July 21, with 67 persons in attendance. The following Sunday
75 members attended the service, and there was so much
encouragement from this response that it was agreed the congregations would continue to meet jointly, alternating among
the churches. This would provide a variety in the worship
experience as well as a place in which the service could be
conducted, since the congregation sponsoring the service on a
respective Sunday would provide the minister for the day. It
was agreed that envelope offerings would go to the designated
congregations and loose offerings to the sponsoring church.

On September 21, 1963, the denominational representatives
met with the negotiating committee to complete the plans for
the proposed unified ministry. The first agreement was to
continue the joint services of worship, and a schedule of these

was adopted. The congregations were continuing the alternate use of buildings.

The UCC representative proposed a budget for financing the project during the two-year experimental period. Each congregation would be asked to contribute to this budget the amount they had been paying for ministerial leadership during the past year. Even with this participation there would be a deficit of $4,000 in the proposed budget for support of the program. The amount of this deficit could be supplied by the United Church Board for Homeland Ministries (UCC) and the Penn West Conference as aid to the project until the budget could be raised locally. This budget was accepted by the negotiating committee for recommendation to the congregations. Each congregation would continue to pay its benevolent monies to its own denomination until a vote to consolidate would be taken.

If the individual congregations should vote to dissolve within the two-year period for the purpose of creating one church, the committee agreed that the resultant congregation would be affiliated with the United Church of Christ. Furthermore, if the congregations voted to become one, the resultant congregation would be considered a *new church*.

Since the Lutheran church was the only congregation to own a house in the community, the committee decided to approach the congregation on the availability of this house for use as a parsonage for the new pastor. For a number of years this house had been allowed to deteriorate, until renovations estimated at about $4,200 were required before it could be used.

The first joint communion service of the four congregations was held on October 6, 1963 (Worldwide Communion Sunday). Attending the service were 150 persons from the community, with 120 receiving Holy Communion. To enhance the true ecumenical spirit of this service, a representative of each denomination served at the Lord's table.

Following the communion service a joint congregational meeting was conducted at which the UCC representative explained the proposals of the unified ministry and the budget. Much enthusiasm permeated the discussion that followed and all the proposals were adopted.

The members of the Lutheran congregation met separately after the other congregations were dismissed and voted to transfer ownership of their parsonage to the Penn West Conference (UCC) so that the Conference could arrange for a local loan to renovate the house. It was understood that if the Lutheran congregation voted not to go into the consolidated church, the house would be deeded back to the congregation, which would then assume any outstanding indebtedness. An item in the adopted budget provided for the repayment of a loan during the experimental period.

On Monday, October 7, 1963, a letter explaining the project and a copy of the budget was mailed to every church member as information.

A Board of Directors Is Appointed

The denominational representatives met with the official boards of each congregation on November 22, 1963, to arrange for a board of directors to be appointed to conduct the affairs of the project during the experimental period. Three representatives of each congregational official board were thus appointed. These directors agreed to meet regularly with the pastor, when appointed, to help guide the work and determine the program. The denominational representatives reported that arrangements for the withdrawal of present ministerial leadership from the community had been agreed to and that all ministers would be withdrawn upon the appointment of a UCC pastor. The UCC pastor who had served up to this point had been called to another parish. The Methodist, Presbyterian, and Lutheran pastors would each have one less congregation to serve, since their parish boundaries would be restructured when the Schellsburg churches would be served by a resident pastor.

The organizational meeting of the board of directors was conducted on December 15, 1963, under the leadership of a representative of the Penn West Conference (UCC). The board elected its own officers—chairman, vice-chairman, secretary, and treasurer. The following agreements were reached:

1. Each congregation should have one alternate member in addition to the regular members on the board of directors.
2. A quorum for the board of directors would be two members from each congregation.
3. A parsonage committee was appointed.
4. The moving expenses of the pastor would be paid.

The directors were informed that the council of the Lutheran congregation objected to the stipulation in the transfer of deed to the parsonage that indicated, in the event the Lutheran congregation voted not to go into the consolidation, the deed would be transferred back to the congregation, which would then assume any unpaid balance of the renovation cost. This objection indicated some concern on the part of the council that the Lutheran members would not vote for a consolidation. They did not want to lose the house that the congregation owned if this would be the case, nor did they want to transfer the deed allowing for renovations for which they might later be responsible. The only recourse for the board of directors was to look for another place to use as a parsonage until this matter could be settled.

Progress with a Pastor

Although the UCC denomination does not have an appointment system for pastors in established congregations, it does have a system of engaging the services of a pastor for a new church when there is no organized congregation to conduct an election. The project at Schellsburg was considered as a mission project during the experimental period. This enabled the denomination, through its Penn West Conference, to appoint a pastor to this field until a new congregation could be organized. On December 19, 1963, the Rev. Daniel G. Kratz accepted the appointment to Schellsburg and agreed to begin his ministry on February 1, 1964. The pastor and his family would move into an apartment in the community until the matter concerning the parsonage could be settled.

On December 30, 1963, the UCC representative met with the board of directors to plan for the arrival of the pastor. The treasurer reported that he had no funds with which to pay any expenses of the joint operation. Each congregation had maintained its own treasury and handled its own funds since the beginning of the joint worship services. This pattern would continue as long as the congregations retained their identities. Since some immediate expenses would be incurred with the arrival of the pastor, it was agreed that each congregation would make available to the treasurer of the board of directors an advance of $50. In addition to this, the church school (which had been union) would contribute approximately $400, and the United Church Board for Homeland Ministries and the Penn West Conference would each advance $500 of the first year's subsidy. This would provide a total of $1,600 on which the board of directors could operate effectively. Joint expenses for such things as ministerial leadership, parsonage rent, pastor's moving expense, and program supplies would be paid from the treasury of the board of directors.

Since the beginning of joint worship services, the congregations had alternated in the use of buildings. The church school materials and extra hymnals had to be carried to a different church each week. Although this saved each congregation some cost in heating, it was confusing and troublesome to the members. On January 22, 1964, the board of directors took a major step forward in the experiment and agreed that all services would be conducted in the UCC building.

When the pastor arrived to begin his ministry on February 1, he was the community's first resident pastor in many years. The apartment that had been rented for him and his family was located on the main street of the community, just a short distance from the church in which the people were worshiping. The apartment was not large enough to provide for a pastor's study and church office. The local bank offered the use of a room in its building, at no cost to the churches, for this purpose.

A further demonstration of the ecumenical spirit of this cooperative effort was evidenced on February 12, 1964, at a special service of recognition for the pastor, his family, and the mission project. An official representative of each denomination participated in this service and publicly named the pastor as supply pastor of his respective congregation with all rights and privileges of a regular pastor of the denomination. This public recognition and official statement on the part of denominational executives made it easier for the pastor to relate to the members of the respective congregations. Following the service the women of all the churches served as hostesses for a reception in honor of the pastor and his family.

When the Lutheran council had taken no action to transfer the deed to the house by March 20, 1964, an overture was made to the Church Building Department of the United Church Board for Homeland Ministries to provide funds for the purchase of another house that could be used as a parsonage. When it was learned that a suitable house was available in the community, the pastor was instructed to submit all the details to the Church Building Department in the request for a loan to purchase it. This proved to be unnecessary, however, because the Lutheran council agreed on April 20, 1964, to follow through on the original plan.

Through the cooperation of the Central Pennsylvania Synod, Lutheran Church in America, an agreement was reached and proceedings to transfer the deed to the Lutheran house to the Penn West Conference (UCC) were commenced. The parsonage committee of the board of directors was asked to determine the needed renovations and to arrange for the beginning of these renovations as soon as the present occupants moved. The Penn West Conference agreed to borrow funds from the local bank for these renovations and to pay the mortgage from the project budget.

Reaching an Early Decision

The denominational representatives fully expected that the project would continue through two years under the leadership of the pastor before further voting of the congregations would be required. When they met with the pastor on June 3, 1964, however, the evidence he presented altered their expectations. The pastor reported the following:

1. More people were attending church in Schellsburg than ever before; average attendance was 132.
2. The giving of the people exceeded all expectations. Projected receipts, based on experience from the first four months, indicated the congregations would contribute approximately $1,000 more than anticipated. The benevolence of each congregation had been paid quarterly from the treasury of the board of directors.
3. The transfer of deed to the Lutheran house was almost complete, and renovations were expected to begin the last of June.
4. The pastor reported that the members were ready to vote on final consolidation.

Agreements reached:

1. That each of the four congregations should vote to dissolve.
2. That each denominational representative would meet with his respective congregation on September 21, 1964, for discussion on the question of dissolution.
3. That in the event each congregation approves the consoli-

dation, a new congregation would be organized as a United Church of Christ congregation.

4. That the resultant congregation would retain ownership of all properties.
5. That the date of October 4, 1964 (Worldwide Communion Sunday) would be set for voting. A representative of each denomination would be present for this service and call the meeting of his congregation to order. A separate ballot box would be provided for each congregation. The voting would be done as an act of worship and the ballots counted following the service.
6. That if a majority vote would be received, a charter membership list would be opened and remain open through November 22, 1964, for signatures of persons desiring to become members of the new congregation. A special service of organization of the new congregation would take place on November 22, 1964.

By working closely with the people in their daily lives, the pastor had illustrated that ecumenicity can be achieved on the local level if it has the support of the denominations, and if the people have the opportunity to share together in their religious experiences.

Plans had to be made for the voting of the congregations. It was important that the members of each congregation have an opportunity to discuss the pending vote and to raise questions to their denominational representatives. Each congregation would have to receive the same information to avoid confusion in understanding. The denominational representatives met in the afternoon on September 21, 1964, to discuss the details of that which would be presented to the four congregations in separate meetings that evening. The Methodist district superintendent explained that it would not be necessary to have the Methodist congregation vote to dissolve but that the congregation would vote to be transferred to the UCC congregation. Anyone from the Methodist congregation who does not wish to remain in the new congregation would then be transferred to the church of his choice. The other congregations (including the United Church of Christ) would vote to dissolve for the purpose of allowing their members to unite with the new congregation. A charter membership list would be opened immediately if the votes were in the affirmative. Anyone signing the charter would be transferred immediately to the new congregation. Those who chose not to sign the charter would have their names carried on the rolls of their respective judicatory until they would request a letter of transfer to the new congregation or some other congregation. These names would be carried by the judicatory for a period of one to two years.

All funds and assets of the congregations would be turned over to the new congregation if the vote would be favorable. The effective date for the dissolution of the congregations and the organization of the new congregation was tentatively scheduled for November 22, 1964.

The congregational meetings in the evening revealed a greater concern on the part of the members than had been evidenced before. The plan for voting was discussed and the creating of a *new congregation* was emphasized. One important question that came from these meetings was: "If one or more churches votes no, what will be their relationship to the churches that go into the consolidation?" It was explained that the pastor would continue as supply pastor for dissenting congregations for the remainder of the two-year period. If at the end of this time the congregation (s) still did not choose to go into the consolidation, the denomination of the congregation (s) would assist it in an orderly dissolution and disposal of the property and assets according to its polity. Under no circumstances would any of the cooperating denominations send a competing minister to Schellsburg following the voting of the congregations.

When the people of Schellsburg came to church on October 4, 1964, they joined with Christians the world over in the observance of worldwide communion. They came also to cast their lots on the question of demonstrating a closer unity in Christ than had ever before been attempted by so many congregations in one community. When all the pews were filled the ushers brought in folding chairs and, as quickly as they were in place, they too were occupied. One was reminded of the narrative of the dedication of the Jerusalem temple, during the dedication of which it was said, "The glory of the Lord filled the house of the Lord" (1 Kings 8:11). As it was said of that day, so could it be said of this.

Of the more than 200 attending this service, including children, 141 came to the altar to partake of the sacrament. They came as one people in a demonstration of their worship and program of more than a year. They came in unity of purpose and fellowship in the Lord.

Following the service of worship, the pastor reconvened the congregational meetings of September 21. His call:

The meeting of the _____ congregation, which was recessed on September 21, is hereby reconvened on October 4, for the purpose of voting on the resolution that was mailed to you.

Representatives of each congregation distributed the ballots, which were printed on a different colored paper for each congregation. When the ballots were marked, the members were asked to proceed to the chancel rail and place their ballots in a matching colored box.

When the voting was completed, the appointed tellers were instructed to count the ballots. Results of the voting were as follows:

Congregation	Total Number Votes	Yes Votes	No Votes	Abstaining
St. Matthews Evangelical Lutheran	16	11	5	0
Schellsburg Methodist	25	23	2	0
Schellsburg Presbyterian	27	14	13	0
St. John's Reformed (UCC)	60	53	5	2
Totals	128	101	25	2

The pastor announced that the vote had carried in all four congregations. The date of November 22, 1964, was given as the organizational date of the new congregation to be organized under the auspices of the United Church of Christ.

Immediately following the announcement, the charter membership list of the new congregation was opened and members began to sign. A name for the new congregation would be chosen on October 11, 1964, and a constitution would soon follow.

The nation descended on the community of Schellsburg on November 22, 1964, and more especially on the United Church there, through reporters and cameramen of newspapers, TV stations, national magazine publications, and denominational and interdenominational representatives. More than

300 persons were in attendance for the formal organizational service of the new Schellsburg United Church of Christ.

Greetings from executives of each denomination represented in the community were extended to the congregation. A representative of the National Council of the Churches of Christ in the U.S.A. delivered the morning address. Representatives of the Pennsylvania Council of Churches expressed their congratulations and appreciation. The total charter membership, made up of persons from all four congregations, numbered 225. As these people were received into membership, nearly four years of negotiations were brought to a close.

Following the impressive morning service, the congregation and invited guests gathered in the community firehall for a fellowship meal, after which the new members returned to the church to adopt a new constitution, extend a unanimous call to the pastor, elect officers, appoint committees, and plan for the future.

The churches of Schellsburg have proven that community planning in church adjustment to meet the needs of a changing society is possible, even across denominational lines. No one really lost anything through this consolidation. It is true that three denominational units ceased to be, but the community achieved a degree of unity through the discussions and ultimate consolidation that had never before been possible. There had been few, if any, active programs in the congregations before this action was taken. One year following the consolidation, the church had achieved a measure of progress evidenced by these facts:

1. A Girl Scout troop with 63 girls and a Boy Scout troop with 50 boys had been organized.
2. The total giving had increased by 25.6 percent over the previous year. Current expenses were up 20.4 percent. Benevolent giving was up 80 percent.
3. The membership had grown by 12 percent during the first year of operation. During this year 35 new members were received, 18 of whom had never belonged to any one of the four congregations when they were in existence.

Shortly after the consolidation of the churches in Schellsburg, a sectarian minister came to the community in the hope of starting another congregation. The agreements of the congregations made it impossible for him to use one of the church buildings in the community; however, he did rent an abandoned school building and started conducting weekly services. The people of Schellsburg were so solidly behind the consolidation that he was unable to develop any membership for his congregation and gave up the attempt after a short time.

This is not the end of the Schellsburg story—only the beginning. Ecumenicity is not just talked about in this community, *it is action, and it is real.* The future offers hope and achievement for these people who, by their vote and practice, have found a oneness in Christ often sought by others.

Chapter Three

✠

United Church of Muscoda—Presbyterian Muscoda, Wisconsin

THERE ARE FEW churches that perform their ministry in isolated situations. Most churches are located so that even in sparsely settled areas there is usually more than one congregation from which the people can choose to attend. Even though there may be theological and governmental differences between the churches in a natural geographical area, there are similar opportunities and problems, and the churches are similarly affected by the social changes around them. Fluctuations in population and economy affect each church that is located in the area of the change. Any change in parish alignment and services rendered by a church may affect the ministry of a neighboring church even though the two churches do not belong to the same denominational family.

The interrelatedness of adjusted ministries has not always been understood by those denominational leaders who have had responsibility for church planning. Adjustments have often been made in response to a particular denominational need and to satisfy a particular denominational concern. Parishes have been aligned denominationally to provide enough units with sufficient resources to support a pastor, while ignoring the needs of other congregations in the area. Denominations have closed churches when the membership was no longer large enough to support a program and when no denominational parish arrangement could be established. Often such adjustments have been made without consultations with other churches or denominational leaders who are also concerned with the same community. Relocations of congregations have been planned without consideration for cooperative strategy.

It is true that the first obligation of a denominational executive is to the congregations of his own fellowship. It is also true that this obligation should extend beyond the congregational unit to the community that the congregation has sought to serve. When there is a need for an adjustment in the ministry of a particular church, there is a need to examine that ministry in the total community context. This examination will naturally involve other churches in the same geographical area. A cooperative examination of the situation, made by the congregations and their denominational leaders, can result in better strategy to meet the needs of the total community.

State and local councils of churches make it possible for denominational leaders to meet together to discuss their common problems and to plan for more effective church adjustment. Many congregations, through their denominational representatives, are asking councils of churches for assistance in making community studies on an interdenominational basis. The information obtained through such studies is then shared with each denomination represented and often results in some cooperative adjustment to strengthen the total religious life of the community.

A Request for Study

The Methodist bishop and an executive of the Presbyterian synod in southwestern Wisconsin submitted such a request to the Department of Research of the Wisconsin Council of Churches for staff assistance in the study of the churches in their area. On May 9, 1963, this request was approved by the Department of Research and plans were made to begin a study of the churches in a 20-mile square area that included three counties. The ultimate objective of such an undertaking was to determine what steps should be taken to provide a more adequate ministry. There was no preconceived plan of adjustment or goal of accomplishment other than that of strengthening church life and enabling the churches of the area to witness more adequately to the unchurched people.

At the request of the Methodist district superintendent and the secretary of the Presbyterian Town and Country Department, all the pastors in the selected area of study from both denominations met on May 31, 1963, to report on the local church situations. Each pastor described the parish he served and the churches under his responsibility, indicating size, location of membership on area maps, extent of congregational witness, facilities, and school district boundaries. From these reports and subsequent discussions, it became evident that the Methodists had problems in some localities and the Presbyterians had problems in others. The one place where both denominations discovered a need for adjustment, and where the council of churches should be involved, was in and around the village of Muscoda (pronounced Mus-co-day).

Muscoda is located forty-five miles east of the Iowa border and fifty-six miles north of the Illinois border. There has been little change in the population since the 1960 census, which reported 927 people. Four churches ministered to the people of the village—St. John the Baptist Roman Catholic Church with 1,030 members (many of whom came from surrounding communities), St. Peter Lutheran Church (Missouri Synod) with 150 baptized members, the Methodist Church with 122 resident adult members, and the First Presbyterian Church with 113 communicant members. In addition, another Presbyterian church was located four miles southeast of Muscoda in the community of Pulaski, and the Methodist denomination had another church at Avoca, seven miles east of Muscoda.

First Meeting Proposals

At the meeting on May 31, the following challenging proposals affecting the Methodist and Presbyterian churches in Muscoda, Pulaski, and Avoca were made:

1. For a stronger witness in Muscoda, with a more adequate pastoral ministry and a more meaningful program by and for the people in Muscoda, there should be one congregation instead of the two that now exist.
2. The membership of the Pulaski Presbyterian congregation should become an integral part of the new Muscoda congregation.

3. The membership of the Avoca Methodist Church should become an integral part of this congregation, or be served by the pastor of this new Muscoda congregation, or be served in some other manner.

These were ambitious proposals to come from a first meeting on area study. What had started as a detailed study of a three-county area was now focused on four congregations in three small communities, with a suggested plan of adjustment that would reduce the number of congregational units from four to one or two units. The proposal to consolidate across denominational lines was even more dramatic considering the fact that no laymen of the congregations were present to express their own views on the matter. Representatives at this meeting recognized the need to involve the laymen in further study and planned for them to be present at the next meeting. A representative of the American Lutheran Church in Avoca would also be invited, since this congregation was located in the area of study.

Pastors and lay delegates from the four Methodist and Presbyterian churches, their denominational leaders, the council of churches representative, and the pastor of the American Lutheran Church in Avoca met on June 27, 1963, to continue the discussion on the future of the churches in the Muscoda area. The Lutheran pastor informed the group that his denomination, prior to his call, had completed a lengthy study of its own churches in the area, which had resulted in a parish realignment. Any further changes would probably not be made in the immediate future. The discussions regarding possible adjustments among the Methodist and Presbyterian churches would continue.

Consideration of a united ministry between the Methodist and Presbyterian churches in Muscoda was not new. In 1940 these two congregations had considered forming a federated church, but that plan had never been brought to fruition. Over the years several union worship services had been held by the two congregations; in 1962 and 1963 they had cooperated in vacation church schools. This was the first time, however, that the members of the Pulaski Presbyterian Church or the Avoca Methodist Church had ever examined their own witness to see if they should continue on the same basis, or if they would be strengthened by joining efforts with the two congregations at Muscoda.

After considering statistical information on the area and discussing possible alternatives, two agreements were made:

1. The session of the First Presbyterian Church and the official board of the Methodist Church in Muscoda should take official action to the effect that they are in favor of the overall proposal for one congregation in Muscoda instead of the two that now exist. It is understood that the new congregation would be related to either denomination but not to both, and that each would be willing to accept whichever denomination the future would bring; that is, the Presbyterians would be willing to become Methodists and the Methodists would be willing to become Presbyterians, in order that a united witness and a united pastoral ministry could be made through one congregation to the people in the Muscoda area.
2. The session of the Pulaski Presbyterian Church and the official board of the Avoca Methodist Church would open the way to receive a delegation to consider how their own witness could best be made in the future; that is, how can either or both of these congregations best witness to the Lord Jesus Christ not only among their present membership but also to the unchurched in the wider community. Should they remain as separate congregations, or should they add their strength to the joint endeavor in Muscoda?

These agreements called for positive action on the part of the official boards of each congregation. The boards of the Muscoda churches would take action on their willingness to become one congregation and be affiliated with either one of the two denominations. The official boards of the Pulaski and Avoca churches would take action only to continue discussions about their future. The congregations would not as yet be approached for a vote on this matter.

The session of the First Presbyterian Church of Muscoda met early in July, 1963, and adopted the following resolutions in response to the proposals that were made at the meeting of June 27:

1. We express approval of a plan of consolidation proposed by the Wisconsin Council of Churches involving our congregation and the Methodist Church of Muscoda.
2. We express our approval, whether the denominational affiliation be Presbyterian or Methodist.
3. We recommend that discussion and study of other churches in the area be continued with the hope that the Pulaski

Presbyterian Church and the Avoca Methodist Church may become integrally related to the proposed new church.

4. We suggest that a special committee be formed whose responsibility will be to present a recommendation to the congregations of the First Presbyterian Church and the Muscoda Methodist Church concerning the denominational alignment of the proposed new church. We feel that this decision should be hammered out not at the local level but by the two official boards.

The official board of the Methodist church was unable to take any action on the proposals during the summer because a quorum of members was not present at any of the called meetings.

When the study committee met on August 20, 1963, the action of the Presbyterian session was reported, and plans were made to determine how these decisions could be implemented —provided that the official board of the Methodist church agreed also to the recommendations. A committee composed of four laymen from each church, their pastors, and the director of field services of the Wisconsin Council of Churches was appointed to consider ways of bringing the consolidation into being.

The official board of the Muscoda Methodist Church met on September 7, 1963, and approved the three proposals on which the session of the Presbyterian church had acted earlier. The 23 to 1 favorable vote of the official board cleared the way for the next important step in the process of consolidation.

The Congregations Take Action

When the study committee met on September 11, its members learned that the executives of both denominations supported the consolidation attempt and were willing to abide by any decisions the local congregations would make. The committee was encouraged by this approval and by the action of the local official boards; however, both congregations would have to vote on the recommendation before consolidation would become a reality.

Realizing that the congregations should receive and vote on the same recommendations, the committee agreed to submit the following three-point resolution to the congregations for their consideration:

1. The congregation of the $\begin{cases} \text{Methodist Church} \\ \text{First Presbyterian Church} \end{cases}$ in Muscoda is in favor of the proposal that there should be one congregation in Muscoda instead of the two that now exist.

2. It is understood that the new congregation will be related to either the Methodist Church or the United Presbyterian Church in the U.S.A., but not to both, and that the present constituency will accept whichever denomination the future will bring.

3. It is understood that if each congregation—with at least a two-thirds majority of the members present—votes in favor of both of the preceding proposals, a study committee will proceed to work out the details; when they have done so, they will submit these to each congregation for final approval.

The meeting for the Methodist congregation was scheduled for Saturday, September 28, 1963, and the meeting for the Presbyterian congregation was called for Sunday, September 29, 1963.

The disposition of property was discussed and the committee agreed (with denominational approval) that if a consolidation would be effected, all property of both congregations would become the property of the new congregation; any property not used by the consolidated church could *not* be rented, sold, or used by any other religious group.

The agreements thus far affected most seriously the Methodist and Presbyterian churches in Muscoda. The Methodist church in Avoca and the Presbyterian church in Pulaski had not been neglected, however. On September 18, 1963, the Madison Presbytery had directed the Pulaski session to make arrangements with the pastor of the First Presbyterian Church of Muscoda or the pastor of the Highland Presbyterian Church, which was the next nearest Presbyterian church, to supply their pulpit. The congregation was also asked to participate in the discussions in Muscoda. If the congregation would not participate in these discussions, they would be given until December 31, 1964, to work out a more permanent pastoral arrangement for their 58 members and to give reasons for continuing as a congregation.

On September 20, a contingent of the study committee of Muscoda met with the official board of the Methodist church at Avoca. After considerable discussion the members of the official board of Avoca concluded that they should maintain their own church there and not go into any consolidation. The congregation at Avoca indicated a willingness on its part to be served by the pastor who would come to Muscoda. The hope was expressed that the Muscoda church would become Methodist.

In accordance with the polity of the Methodist discipline, a congregational meeting was conducted in the Methodist Church in Muscoda on September 28, 1963. Unanimous approval by the nineteen members present was given to the three motions adopted for presentation at the September 11 meeting. The following day, which was Sunday, the Presbyterian congregation met and voted on the same resolutions. The results were as follows:

44 Yes   2 No   1 Void   1 Undecided

The committee later recognized that Saturday evening was a poor time for a congregational meeting to consider questions of this nature. Many members of the Methodist congregation who on September 7 had approved the recommendation of the May 31 meeting felt there was no need to vote again on the same proposals and therefore did not attend the Methodist congregational meeting.

Plans and Decisions on Denomination

The committee met on October 3, 1963, to determine what steps should be taken to complete the consolidation. A review of the congregations' legal papers pertaining to property, and the constitutions and charters indicated no outstanding obligations of either congregation that would be a barrier to consolidation.

The choice of denominational affiliation for the new church yet to be constituted was of immediate importance. The committee did not want to assume responsibility for this decision. The unanimous opinion of the committee was that this decision should be reached by persons outside the community. They therefore decided to form a special committee on denominational alignment, consisting of three voting members who were neither Methodist nor Presbyterian, and two advisory members who had no voting privileges. The voting members appointed to the special committee were the director of field services of the Wisconsin Council of Churches, the chairman of the Department of Research of the council, and the president of the Wisconsin Conference of the United Church of Christ.

Official sanction for the consolidation was given by the Presbytery of Madison on October 14, 1963, when it passed the following resolutions:

1. That presbytery concur with the proposal that there should be one congregation in Muscoda instead of the two that now exist; furthermore, that presbytery approve the continuation of discussions by the study committee.
2. That a special committee be appointed to work out specific details in cooperation with the study committee, to give guidance and counsel to this committee, and to bring back formal and specific recommendations to this judicatory.

The five persons who had been asked to serve on the special committee to determine denominational affiliation accepted their appointment, but raised two important questions for the full study committee to consider:

1. If the decision is made entirely by those outside either denomination, what answer will you give to those who, from within each denomination, may ask, "Why were the denominations who are most involved not a party to the decision? Is it fair that they are merely spectators?"
2. If the staff person from the Wisconsin Council of Churches is a party to the decision and a tie develops so that he casts the tie-breaking vote, what effect will this have on his usefulness to the present two denominations, as well as to the other member denominations?

These questions reflect concern on the part of denominational leaders and council of churches representatives that planning for local church adjustment should not be done entirely by those outside the denomination (s) most affected. The members of the special committee were saying by their question: If a denomination is going to lose a congregation through a consolidation adjustment, that denomination should have a voice in the decision.

During this period of time the pastors met and agreed on a schedule of joint worship services, which would be recommended to the study committee for approval. The schedule proposed joint services on special occasions, such as Easter, Christmas Eve, New Year's Eve, World Day of Prayer, Youth

Week, midweek lenten services, and Good Friday. The pastors also recommended that the congregations begin worshiping together regularly in April, 1964, and that they begin functions as one congregation by mid-June, 1964.

When the study committee met on October 25, 1963, the report of the action of the Presbytery of Madison was received, and the questions of the special committee on denominational alignment were discussed. The wisdom of having denominational representatives assist in the decision of denominational affiliation was quickly recognized and the decision was made to include as voting members of this special committee the formerly named advisory members who represented the Methodist and Presbyterian denominations. The study committee instructed its special committee on denominational alignment to report only their final decision.

The suggested schedule of joint worship services, proposed by the pastors, was examined. The committee asked the pastors to work on another plan for joint worship services that would be held during January, 1964, and be continued until the merger would be completed. A decision on which building would be used for worship was not reached at this time. It was agreed that the educational groups of the two congregations should meet to discuss and make plans for a joint church school beginning the first Sunday in January, 1964.

On November 17, 1963, the pastors presented their revised schedule of joint worship services to the study committee, designating special services to be conducted on Thanksgiving Eve and Christmas Eve, with regular Sunday morning joint services to begin on January 5, 1964. The committee agreed that the services would be held on two consecutive Sundays in one church, the pastor of that church conducting the service and the organist of that church playing, followed by two weeks in the other church on the same basis. The choirs would combine and all services would be held at 10:00 A.M., beginning on January 5 in the Methodist church. The first combined communion service would be held in Holy Week, celebrated according to the practice of the denomination selected. The offering received at the church worship service would go to the respective congregations by using separate envelope systems. Loose offerings would be divided equally between the two congregations.

The educational subcommittee reported that a combined

teaching staff for the church school was organized and would teach the combined classes beginning January 5 at 9:00 A.M. It was agreed that the United Church of Christ curriculum would be used for the first quarter of 1964, then the material of the chosen denomination would be used for the next quarter. Church school would be held in the same building as the joint worship service. It was further agreed that the joint church school should have a separate treasury and treasurer; the treasury would consist of all freewill offerings, and all expenses would be paid from this treasury.

The question of the ownership of the Methodist parsonage in Muscoda was raised. Concern was expressed over whether or not the Avoca Methodist Church had some interest in this property. A representative was delegated to look into the matter and report on it the following month.

The first meeting of the special committee on denominational alignment was conducted on November 24, 1963. After examining the available facts the committee decided that more information was needed. A questionnaire was drawn up to be sent to all members of both congregations, along with a request that the questions be answered and returned in postage-prepaid envelopes to the office of the director of field service of the Wisconsin Council of Churches. A tabulation of the answers would be made from this office and shared with the other four members of the special committee. The results of the questionnaire would be confidential—used only by the special committee.

A union memorial service for the late President Kennedy was conducted on March 25, 1964.

The special committee on denominational alignment reported to the study committee on December 13, 1963, regarding the questionnaire. After discussion on the wording of the questionnaire and the need for it, the study committee agreed that it should be distributed to all the members of the congregations with the request that it be mailed to Madison, Wisconsin, by December 31.

Reporting on the study made of the ownership of the Methodist parsonage in Muscoda, the representative of the committee stated that the parsonage, in his opinion, was owned jointly and equally by the Muscoda Methodist Church and the Avoca Methodist Church. The study committee authorized the appointment of three representatives from each of these

Methodist congregations to report further on this matter at the next meeting.

For publicity purposes the committee agreed that a temporary name should be given to the new venture of the two congregations. The name The United Church of Muscoda was selected until a permanent name could be officially established.

A suggestion was made that one of the church buildings should be moved beside the other so that the two structures would be joined together. Since there was no immediate need to consider this, the suggestion was tabled.

A discussion ensued regarding a pastor for the new church. It was agreed that neither of the present pastors should be the first pastor of the United Church of Muscoda.

It was reported that the Pulaski Presbyterian session had been visited and that the session had indicated a lack of interest on the part of their people in becoming a part of a merged congregation at this time. The thought was expressed that they might be interested in being supplied by the pastor who might serve the new church in Muscoda.

The questionnaires that were given to every member, having been returned and tabulated, were distributed in advance to the members of the special committee on denominational alignment, which met on January 15, 1964, to give further consideration to their tasks. Two hundred and twenty-two questionnaires were distributed, with 147 being returned. Some of the principal questions and results were as follows:

- Would you find it difficult to change to the other denomination involved in this merger?
                Answer—3 to 1—No.
- When this merger is completed will you happily be a member of it?
                Answer—8 to 1—Yes.
- Which denomination would you prefer?
                Answer—1 out of 4—No preference.

It was agreed that no definite decision on denominational affiliation should be made at the meeting, but that each member should prayerfully consider the whole matter and mail his vote to the office of the Wisconsin Council of Churches on February 19, so that it would arrive on February 20. The results of this voting would be revealed in Muscoda on February 23, when all members of the special committee could be present.

The Pulaski Presbyterian Church was still struggling with a decision about its own future. At the annual meeting of this congregation in January, 1964, the members expressed a desire to have a meeting with the director of field services of the Wisconsin Council of Churches sometime in March. The reasons for choosing this month for a meeting were given as follows:

1. The denominational decision of the Muscoda church would be made by then.
2. They would like to have consideration as a possible second congregation to be served by the pastor who would come to the United Church of Muscoda.

When the study committee met on January 19, 1964, the members enthusiastically received the report on attendance at the joint worship services. One hundred and eighty-five people had attended the first service on January 5, and attendance at the succeeding services had leveled off to about 150. The church school sessions had been well-attended and no problems were apparent. A full staff was at work in the church school.

The special committee on denominational alignment presented certain positive suggestions concerning the handling of property which the study committee accepted for further study. The study committee was also encouraged to stress the real goal it hoped to achieve through the consolidation, that goal being a better and stronger witness in the community, including the Pulaski and Avoca areas.

A report was given by the special committee on the Methodist parsonage ownership. The report confirmed the original statement, which indicated that the Muscoda church and the Avoca church shared equally in this property. To make this official for the Methodist church, the rules of paragraph 184 of the *Discipline of the Methodist Church* would have to be followed. This meant that the Methodist district superintendent would have to appoint a committee from outside the parish to examine the information; then he would make his recommendations. It was hoped that this could be expeditiously handled.

How could the recommendation of the special committee on

denominational alignment be communicated to the two congregations as soon as possible and then brought to a vote?
After considerable deliberation the study committee decided
to call special congregational meetings of both congregations
at 8 P.M. on February 23, for the purpose of receiving the
report of the denominational alignment committee and voting
on the denomination that the committee had agreed to recommend. It was agreed that a two-thirds majority of the members
present and voting would be necessary for passage in each
congregation. Each congregation was to use ballots of a different color.

On January 29, 1964, the supply pastor of the Pulaski Presbyterian Church announced that he had accepted a call to
another parish. The members of the Pulaski church session
expressed a desire to discuss their congregation's future with
the Ministerial Relations Committee of Madison Presbytery before their scheduled March meeting with the director of field
services of the Wisconsin Council of Churches. They also
expressed a strong desire to maintain their own congregational
identity and to use their own building for worship, all of
which they wanted to discuss with the Presbytery.

A meeting of a special committee on the matter of ownership of the Methodist parsonage was called by the Methodist
district superintendent on February 8, 1964. The committee
concurred with the conclusion of the local committee; namely,
that the parsonage was owned jointly and equally by the two
congregations. If Avoca were not to be part of the consolidation, and if the new united church should want to make use
of the Muscoda parsonage after the proposed consolidation, it
would be clearly understood that the Avoca Methodist Church
had one-half interest in this building and one-half responsibility for it, whatever the future might bring.

The Methodist and Presbyterian youth groups met early in
February, 1964, and agreed to merge. New officers were elected
and a plan for weekly meetings was set forth. An adult counselor for the group was secured.

The study committee met on February 23, 1964, an hour
before the specially called congregational meetings, to set up
an agenda for these meetings. The pastors had submitted a
suggested procedural outline, which the committee approved.
If both congregations in their concurrent meetings voted favor-

ably on the resolution to form one church, it was agreed that there should be a meeting of the new united congregation for the purpose of electing a nominating committee. This committee would nominate persons for the official board of the new congregation and set a date for the nominating committee to report. It was agreed that the judicatory representative of the denomination chosen should preside over the latter meeting of the new congregation and would be responsible for planning with the new congregation. However, the director of field services of the Wisconsin Council of Churches would continue to participate in the development as adviser and observer until the actual merger would take place. This was the final meeting of the study committee.

The congregations met together in the Methodist church at 8 p.m. for a brief devotional period before the official meetings of each congregation were called to order.

The all-important recommendation of the special committee on denominational affiliation was presented to the members. Each of the five members of the committee had voted separately on the recommendation by mail and the report given to the congregations indicated that the committee was unanimous in recommending that the consolidation take place, and that the united congregation be affiliated with the United Presbyterian Church in the U.S.A.

Officials of both denominations had been consulted earlier so that proper resolutions could be prepared for the official voting regardless of what the recommendation of the special committee might be. The duplicate resolutions required a simple yes-no marking by the members.

A resolution of eleven paragraphs in which all the information necessary to dissolve both present congregations and form the United Church of Muscoda–Presbyterian was read to the congregations. This resolution, which had been prepared by the study committee, was discussed and then voted upon.

Following the practice of the Methodist denomination, the members of the Methodist Quarterly Conference received and marked their ballots first. These were counted by the appointed tellers; the district superintendent revealed that the vote was satisfactory and that the members of the Methodist church could therefore proceed to vote on the same question.

All qualified voters of the two congregations present at the meeting received ballots that were identical in content, but different in color. Following the voting and during the tabulation, a question arose about property. It was stated by representatives of both judicatories that all property owned by the two congregations would become the property of the united church with the exception of the one-half interest in the Methodist parsonage that was owned by the Avoca Methodist Church.

The following results of the voting were reported by the tellers:

	Yes	*No*
Methodist Quarterly Conference	17	1
Methodist congregation	33	3
Presbyterian congregation	48	3

Organizing for Unity

When the concurrent congregational meetings were adjourned—there being no reason to believe that all present would not elect to be a part of the consolidated church—the members were reconvened to meet under the name of the United Church of Muscoda–Presbyterian. A member of the study committee who had served throughout the discussion was elected to serve the new congregation as clerk. A previously prepared petition to the Presbytery of Madison requesting permission to be constituted and organized as a new congregation of that denomination was passed. The actual consolidation would take place officially on June 15, 1964. Both the Methodist and Presbyterian congregations would continue in existence until that time.

Nominations from the floor brought the election of six persons to the nominating committee, which included three from each of the constituting congregations. This committee was charged with the responsibility of nominating members for the session and the board of deacons for the new congregation. It was agreed that each of these bodies should consist of twelve people. The committee was to present its slate of nominees at the next meeting of the congregation, which was scheduled for April 5, 1964.

A question was raised about a pulpit committee. Since the members of such a committee need time to understand one another, and since the members of the former study committee had displayed their ability along this line, it was suggested that they be considered as the nucleus of the pulpit committee. This suggestion was put in the form of a motion and duly passed. When it was pointed out that Presbyterian polity requires a representative of the youth organization to be a member of this pulpit committee, the congregation promptly elected the leader of this organization to serve with the others already named.

The nominating committee met on March 15, 1964, and reviewed the duties and standards of church officers according to Presbyterian polity. The committee then prepared a list of twenty-four names to recommend to the congregation as officers of the new church. The term of office would begin on the organization date of the congregation. Of these twenty-four names, twelve were suggested for the office of elder and twelve for the office of deacon. Half the number suggested were from the Methodist church and half were from the Presbyterian. It was agreed that each nominee would be contacted by the committee prior to the election by the congregation to determine his willingness to serve in the capacity suggested.

The spirit of unity grew throughout special joint services conducted during Holy Week. On March 25, 1964, the first joint Holy Communion service was observed. On March 27 the president of the Wisconsin Conference of the United Church of Christ was the guest speaker for a Good Friday afternoon service. The youth fellowship conducted an Easter Sunrise service at 6 A.M. on March 29. This service was followed by breakfast. Although the attendance was not large, it was a meaningful experience for those who did attend. Two other joint services were conducted that morning at 8 A.M. and 10 A.M. Each pastor led one of the services. A total of 240 persons attended.

The meeting between the director of field services of the Wisconsin Council of Churches and the session of the Pulaski Presbyterian Church, scheduled for March, had to be postponed until April 1, 1964. Although no formal action was taken, the session examined its alternatives in the light of its efforts to continue its own separate ministry. These alternatives were given as follows:

1. A form of permanent supply ministry by the pastor at Muscoda Church or the pastor of the Highland Presbyterian Church.

2. Their actual agreement with one of these congregations
   jointly to call a pastor.

There were strong sentiments toward working with the Highland Church rather than with the Muscoda Church because an
arrangement with the Highland Church posed no threat to
the Pulaski witness. This meeting helped the people to clarify
their thoughts and determine a direction that assured them
continuation as a congregation.

The National Missions Committee of the Madison Presbytery met on April 2, 1964, and accepted the action taken by the
congregations on February 23. A seven-point resolution was
drafted for action by the Presbytery to clear the way for
consummation of the consolidation.

A concern was expressed over the future of the Presbyterian
pastor in Muscoda. The relocation of the Methodist pastor
would not be difficult to achieve in the Methodist procedure.
However, the Presbyterian procedure is more complex. The
Ministerial Relations Committee of the Presbytery presented a
request to meet with the pulpit committee of the United
Church of Muscoda with the hope that the present Presbyterian pastor could serve the congregation on an interim basis
until he received a suitable call.

For the first time since the congregations had met jointly for
worship, a unified form of service—as recommended in the
Presbyterian *Book of Common Worship*—was used on April 5,
1964. It was agreed that this form of service would be used
each Sunday even though the congregations would continue
for the present to alternate in the use of buildings.

The Presbyterian church school curriculum was introduced
for use in the church school at this time. After the favorable
vote on February 23 this material was ordered and the teachers
were prepared to use it. Although the United Church of
Christ material was used for only one quarter, it served to
unite the combined staffs with their pupils preparatory to the
use of the material of their new denomination.

A special congregational meeting was conducted in the evening of April 5 to receive the report of the nominating committee. The committee presented its slate of names for the
following offices:

> 12 elders to serve on the session
> 12 trustees to serve as deacons
> treasurer
> secretary

Six persons were nominated from each congregation for the office of elder, and six members from each church for the office of trustee. A Presbyterian was nominated for treasurer and a Methodist was nominated for secretary. Although the new officers would serve in no official capacity until the new congregation was actually organized, it was agreed that they should prepare themselves to assume their duties. The officers of the two congregations would continue to serve until the organization date.

The Madison Presbytery met on April 15, 1964, and received the resolution presented by its National Missions Committee. The resolution was joyfully adopted by the Presbytery, making it possible for the First Presbyterian Church of Muscoda to be dissolved on June 15, and to organize a new congregation to be known as the United Church of Muscoda–Presbyterian on the same date. Title of all real property of the old congregations would be transferred to the new congregation as of June 15. It was understood that all members of both congregations who make no requests for transfer prior to that date would become charter members of the new congregation.

The request of the Ministerial Relations Committee of the Presbytery to meet with the pulpit committee of the United Church of Muscoda was presented. It was the hope of the pulpit committee that the Presbyterian pastor would serve the United Church as interim pastor until he would receive a suitable call. The Presbytery concurred with this request.

The education committee met on April 17, 1964, to plan for a vacation church school. The committee outlined plans for having the prospective teachers of this school attend a training institute on April 30.

The Ministerial Relations Committee of the Presbytery met with the church session-elect to discuss its recommendations concerning the Presbyterian pastor. The session-elect agreed that this pastor should serve as an interim supply pastor while the church seeks a permanent pastor and he seeks a new position. It was agreed that the matter would be reviewed by the Presbytery at its September meeting.

The church session-elect met on April 24, 1964, to consider matters pertaining to the property, especially the parsonage, which was owned jointly by the Avoca and Muscoda Methodist congregations. The new United Church of Muscoda hoped to be able to purchase full ownership of this parsonage.

The church session-elect, after evaluating the alternating

schedule of services in the two buildings, agreed that the long-term interests would be better served if the Methodist building would be used on a permanent basis. It was decided that both worship and church school would be conducted in this building on a regular basis beginning May 3. It was further agreed that the organ owned by the First Presbyterian Church should be used by the united church.

A special congregational meeting was called following the morning worship service on May 3, 1964. The congregation voted to petition the Madison Presbytery for permission to borrow up to $5,000 to be used to purchase the Avoca Methodist congregation's share of the parsonage.

A joint meeting of the church session-elect and the official boards of the Avoca Methodist and Muscoda Methodist Churches was conducted on May 6, 1964, to consider the purchase of full ownership in the parsonage by the united church. It was agreed that the united church would purchase the Avoca Methodist congregation's share in the parsonage for $2,400. It was understood that the united church would get the electric stove and refrigerator now in the parsonage and that the Avoca Methodist Church would get the mimeograph machine.

Authorization was given at this meeting to engage an architect for a professional opinion on needed improvements to the Methodist building.

The last Quarterly Conference for the Methodist church was convened by the district superintendent on May 18, 1964. It was decided that all records of the congregations should be completed by June 1, 1964.

The Madison Presbytery met and designated an Administrative Commission to Muscoda. This commission was charged with the responsibility of determining that all legal procedures involved in the dissolution of the First Presbyterian Church of Muscoda would be correct, that all requirements on both Methodist and Presbyterian sides would be met, and that the new congregation would be properly constituted on June 15.

The Administrative Commission of the Presbytery met with the church session-elect to prepare the proper procedures to complete this constitution. Corrected membership lists of each congregation were presented to the commission by the two pastors. These lists constituted the charter membership list of the new congregation.

After spending some time on legal matters, the commission members shared their understanding of the responsibilities of deacons and elders with those present. It was decided to provide each of the officers-elect with a copy of the Presbyterian constitution.

Final plans were made for the formal service of organization on June 15.

When the West Wisconsin Conference of the Methodist Church met in St. Luke's Methodist Church, La Crosse, on June 10, 1964, the district superintendent presented the matter of the dissolution of the Muscoda Methodist Church and the recommendation that the property of the congregation be transferred to the Madison Presbytery for eventual transfer to the United Church of Muscoda–Presbyterian. Several questions pertaining to clarification of procedures were raised and answered. The Conference voted unanimously to adopt the recommendations.

The director of field services of the Wisconsin Council of Churches spoke to the Conference on the significance of the consolidation to the state of Wisconsin. Following these remarks the Methodist bishop addressed the Conference to emphasize his personal joy and thankfulness, for out of this consolidation might come a better witness to Jesus Christ in Muscoda. The bishop commended the members of the two congregations for their spirit of cooperation, and the Wisconsin Council of Churches for its role as a helpful, neutral enabler in the process.

The special organizational service of the United Church of Muscoda–Presbyterian was held on June 15, 1964, under the auspices of the Madison Presbytery's Administrative Commission. This service consummated the consolidation in Muscoda and established as official that which had been unofficial. All those present signed the covenant of organization and became official members of the new united church. The nominated elders and deacons were duly elected and officially installed in their respective offices. Elders and deacons who had not already been ordained were now set apart by this act. An official pulpit committee was nominated and elected to serve. The United Church of Muscoda–Presbyterian was born.

Since the Consolidation

With the help of thirty women from both of the former congregations, the Methodist parsonage was renovated for church school use. The Administrative Committee of the Presbytery met to complete its work on the transfer of property. The pulpit committee began its task to seek a new pastor for the congregation. A list of available prospects for the pastorate was provided by the National Placement Bureau in Columbus, Ohio.

The Presbyterian pastor served the congregation as interim supply pastor until September 6, 1964, when he left to begin a course of graduate studies at the University of Wisconsin, in Madison. Until a new pastor could be elected by the congregation, the pulpit would be supplied by members of the faculty of Dubuque Seminary. When a new pastor is elected, another chapter will begin in the life of the United Church of Muscoda–Presbyterian.

Chapter Four

✛

United Community Church (Methodist) Broadlands, Illinois

SOME STATE COUNCILS of churches, through which many Protestant denominational groups find an avenue of working cooperatively, are developing strategy for the adequate churching of America's communities. Such strategy has long been recognized in the many states where comity allocations assure a new community that it will have adequate churches, but not be overchurched by the participating groups. Newer strategy is being developed and employed in the older and usually smaller communities where overchurching is already a reality and a serious problem.

The number of congregations existent in the small communities of this country, the constant shifting of the population, the declining membership of the congregations, and the yoked-parish arrangements, which are sometimes necessary, are prime examples of the need for greater concentration on joint planning for church adjustments in such communities. Planning and concern for cooperative adjustments will, without doubt, enhance the total church's program.

The Illinois Council of Churches has been successful in facing this problem through the cooperation of the participating denominational groups. A suggested procedure for uniting churches (see chapter 8) has been adopted and is now being followed in many communities throughout the state where overchurching is synonymous with weak congregations. Whenever a request for information on church adjustment is received, the council of churches and the state executives of denominations are prepared to fulfill that request through community meetings and planning. A follow-through on these meetings has resulted in a better understanding on the part of local church members, a degree of closer cooperation, and sometimes even an organic union of congregations.

A Request Is Made

Early in 1964 a request for assistance came to the Illinois Council of Churches from the church members in the predominantly farming community of Broadlands, Illinois. There the Methodist, Evangelical United Brethren, and United Church of Christ congregations, each of which was in a parish arrangement with one or more congregations in other communities, ministered as faithfully as possible in their separate ways to the 344 people of Broadlands. The population of the community was comparatively stable—333 in 1950, 344 in 1960, and 350 in 1965. Industry was not expected to locate in the area to cause an improvement in the economy and an increase in the population. The people, therefore, were concerned about establishing a more effective witness for the Lord in the community as it existed. A close survey of the congregational membership and parish alignment of each church was sufficient to convince the residents that these conditions could not long continue without cutting further into the effectiveness of their ministries.

Two ministers lived in the Broadlands community but, because of ministerial responsibilities elsewhere, were able only to give part-time service to the Broadlands congregations. The Methodist pastor served also a Methodist congregation in Longview, Illinois, approximately six miles west of Broadlands, and another congregation in Allerton, Illinois, approximately three miles east of Broadlands. The United Church of Christ pastor shared his time and energies with another congregation in Sidney, Illinois, approximately five miles north of Broadlands. The Evangelical United Brethren pastor lived in Longview and commuted to Broadlands as often as possible to serve his congregation there.

Each congregation owned and maintained its own house of worship, and both the Methodist and United Church of Christ congregations owned parsonages. Membership in the congregations (Methodist 101; Evangelical United Brethren 56; United Church of Christ 74) was not large enough to maintain full and meaningful programs in each congregation.

The ratio of churches to population, with the accompanying difficulties of ministry that prompted the people of Broadlands to take a close look at themselves, exists in hundreds of communities throughout America. Many congregations in such communities accept these circumstances as divine will or judgment that requires of them the continuation of a struggle to protect their particular witness. For many, the withdrawal of a particular denominational influence, the dissolution of a congregation, or consolidation into a unified ministry is considered to be disrespectful to the past and an acknowledgment of failure on the part of the generation that permits such an adjustment to happen. It is often true, therefore, that the weaker a congregation becomes and the more difficulty it has in the performance of its ministry, the more determined its members are to hold on to their congregational identity. Such efforts are commendable from the standpoint of faithfulness to the past and devotion to a particular set of ideals; however, the reality of each situation must be faced if the religious witness in these communities is to be vital.

Facing these realities is not an easy endeavor, for it requires the congregations to think beyond contented familiarity to the broader scope of mission. The needs of the community's religious life must take precedence over the desires of an individual group. The determination of community needs becomes, therefore, both the responsibility and the opportunity of each congregation represented. When representatives of each congregation realize that the needs are greater than the ability of the congregations separately to fulfill them, a climate conducive to change is created. Such realizations come only when there is openness to conversation—and then only when those involved in the conversations are bold enough to accept new ideas. A preconceived solution to the problems of a community's religious life can immediately create a barrier beyond which those who have not been involved in the plan for the solution will not cross. A prerequisite of any conversations of this importance is for those who become actively involved, to maintain an open mind on the outcome of their endeavors.

The people of Broadlands recognized these essentials. The

congregations of Broadlands realized, too, that they did not stand alone in their need for change. The surrounding communities, with whom the Broadlands churches were closely related through their pastors, would unquestionably be affected by any adjustment the Broadlands congregations would make. It was, therefore, with a concern for the total area of churches that in February, 1964, representatives of the Church Planning and Development Commission of the Illinois Council of Churches, denominational executives, pastors, and selected key laymen of each congregation in the communities of Broadlands, Sidney, Longview, and Allerton met to discuss the problems that the churches were facing in each of these communities. The meeting was conducted in Urbana, Illinois, and the procedures set forth by the Church Planning and Development Commission for such an introductory meeting were followed (see chapter 8). Statistical information on population changes, church membership, and parish arrangements was presented and thoroughly discussed.

Discussions Are Begun

After this initial approach, sufficient interest was created among the people of Broadlands to begin serious discussions in the community about the future of the church there. The pastors of the three congregations, the Methodist district superintendent, the Evangelical United Brethren district superintendent, the United Church of Christ conference minister, and the official boards of each congregation met on November 23, 1964, to consider the advisability of starting conversations on a possible consolidation of the three congregations. So that the group could meet on neutral ground, the meeting was conducted in the Broadlands High School building. Having been given a period of time in which information and hopes were freely shared, the participants were convinced that the talks should continue and that each denominational executive would support the effort of the people of the community.

The approval of the denominational executive is essential in negotiations that may result in the loss of a congregation to the denomination. It is advisable to obtain this approval under any circumstances. In some communions the congregation does not own the property it uses in its program; the property belongs to the denomination. Any change affecting the property thereby requires judicatory action. In some communions, even the approval of the executive is not sufficient to permit a congregation to commit itself to a consolidation effort. This approval must also come by judicatory action. However, when the executive does give his approval, as in this instance, the denomination usually accepts his recommendation.

The representatives decided to arrange for joint worship services to be held before making any definite decisions on consolidation. The worship services were planned for the first three Sundays in January, 1965. The services were to be rotated among the churches and each pastor was asked to share in them as his schedule would permit.

The conviction that one church in the community was the answer to the problems of the congregations was so strong during this meeting, it was considered advisable to approach the congregations immediately on the idea. The fourth Sunday in January, 1965, was designated for individual congregational meetings. The plan called for an opinion vote in each congregation to determine the willingness of the people to continue to work toward a consolidation. A steering committee of three persons from each congregation was appointed to work out the details of the consolidation, if such seemed possible.

Most groups that are working toward an adjustment requiring drastic action of a congregation are more cautious in their approach to the people, even on opinion votes, than the action of this group indicates. This attempt to know immediately the feeling of the people illustrates the confidence the official boards and pastors had in their consolidation plans. It also indicates that the people of the community had close relationships through their congregations. Normally, a period of time in which the congregations are given an opportunity to discuss the need for consolidation, as well as to meet for joint worship services, precedes any request for voting.

The steering committee believed that information—more than simply an indication of the willingness of the people to discuss consolidation—would be needed when the congregations met. The people would want to know how the details of such a plan would be worked out. They would want to know about the denominational affiliation, the ministerial leadership, the property, and numerous other factors. When the committee met on December 8, 1964, it considered its task to be that of providing answers to these questions. The committee agreed to formulate a plan of union, which would be shared with the congregations in their respective meetings on January 24, 1965. The denominational executives were asked to assist the committee in this task. The committee began its work by outlining the concerns that would be included in the plan of union.

A. Voting
   1. What percentage of votes would be necessary to effect a consolidation?
   2. What would be the age limit for voting?
   3. Should ballots be given to all members or only resident members?
   4. What would be the date for voting?
B. Property
   1. Which buildings would be used by the consolidated church?
   2. How would the determination be made for the disposal of unused property?
C. Denominational Affiliation
   What procedure would be followed for determining the denominational affiliation?
D. Pastoral Administration
   Would the consolidated congregation be assured of the services of a pastor at the time of the consolidation?

From this outline the committee agreed to recommend the following proposals:

1. Anyone 16 years of age and older and a member of any of the congregations in Broadlands would be permitted to vote.
2. June 1, 1965, would be suggested as the effective date of union.

The chairman of the steering committee appointed a three-member subcommittee on property to evaluate the property of the three congregations and make recommendations regarding the use of the property by the consolidated congregation, if such consolidation would be effected. The subcommittee on property was instructed to submit a report to the steering committee for consideration at its next meeting.

As the date for the congregational meetings approached, the steering committee met on January 19, 1965, to bring together its recommendations to the congregations. These recommendations were detailed in a formal document that would be presented to the congregations as the plan of union. On the basis of these recommendations the congregations would be asked to give an opinion vote on the continuation of discussions. The following is the text of the plan:

Recommendations for Uniting Broadlands Churches
(Plan of Union)

Condition 1: Dates
A. That the date of March 4, 1965, be the date for individual congregational voting on the union.
B. That the date of July 1, 1965, be the tentative date for the completion of the union.

Condition 2: Voting
A. That the minimum age for members voting be 16 years of age.
B. That a straw vote (to register opinion) precede the definite congregational vote.
C. That a two-thirds majority be necessary to approve decision for union.
D. That eligible voters be enrolled members of each church involved and that friends or supporters of the churches be given voice (and/or straw vote) but not definite vote.
E. That announcement of date, place, and procedure of the voting be sent to all nonresident members and resident shut-ins and that ballots for absentee voting be granted upon request.

Condition 3: Property
A. That the property and possessions of the three church bodies remain the property and possessions of the new church union. (The three conferences had granted this assurance.)
B. That the present United Church of Christ parsonage serve as the parsonage for the new union; that the present Methodist church building serve as the worship center for the new union; and that the present Methodist parsonage serve as facilities for Christian education (and other designated activities) for the new union.
C. That the new church union designate its own procedure for disposing of unused property.

Condition 4: Denominational Affiliation
A. That each congregation vote without reference to denominational affiliation.
B. That the matter of denominational affiliation be referred to the Commission of Planning and Development of the Illinois Council of Churches and that their recommendation be accepted with congregational approval.

Condition 5: Pastoral Administration

A. That the present pastors aid in laying as much of the ground-
work as possible if union is approved.

B. That there be provided a pastor who is ready to assume responsibilities at the time when complete union is a reality.

Condition 6: Name

That each of the three communions give ample consideration
to a name for the church and in due time approve a selection
from a list, such as:

1. Christ Church, Broadlands, Illinois
2. Calvary Church, Broadlands, Illinois
3. Peace Church, Broadlands, Illinois
4. Broadlands Union Church, Broadlands, Illinois
5. Broadlands Community Church, Broadlands, Illinois
6. Broadlands Covenant Church, Broadlands, Illinois
7. Trinity Church, Broadlands, Illinois
8. Others can be added
   (with denominational affiliation in small letters in each
   case above)

Although not officially acted upon, it was generally agreed
that unused property would not be sold or rented to another
Protestant church group. Another Protestant group at work in
Broadlands would defeat the purpose of the church consolidation.

The denominational executives assured the committee that
each of the present pastors would continue to serve the respective congregations until the date of consolidation, if consolidation would be effected. According to the Methodist and
Evangelical United Brethren practices, these two pastors
would be appointed to other pastorates as a normal process.
The United Church of Christ pastor was assured the assistance
of the conference minister in relocation. (The United Church
of Christ does not have a policy of pastor appointment.) A
new pastor for the consolidated congregation would be either
appointed by the denomination or called by the congregation,
depending on the ultimate denominational affiliation.

A Move Toward Union

The three congregations held joint worship services on the
first three Sundays in January, 1965. These services were well
attended and helped to create enthusiasm for a better adjustment in the church facilities in the community. On January

24, 1965, when each congregation met in its own building, the people were prepared to listen to the proposal of the official boards and the steering committee. The recommendations for uniting Broadlands churches (plan of union) were distributed and thoroughly discussed at the congregational meetings. Each of the three congregations subsequently voiced approval of the recommendations and authorized the continuation of discussions.

The steering committee could now move ahead in planning for a joint meeting of the congregations, which had been proposed in the plan of union. This meeting was scheduled for March 4, 1965. The purpose of the meeting was to decide the question of consolidation by congregational vote. However, the congregations would be asked to take a straw vote on the question before voting on the official ballot. The committee considered the straw vote to be a means of providing an opportunity for the friends and supporters who were not official members of the congregations to register an unofficial opinion, and indicating the predominant opinion of all concerned persons before the actual vote. The committee agreed that an official vote would be taken regardless of the outcome of the straw vote.

The request for straw votes of the members on a question as important as this is not generally a recommended procedure. Some committees are anxious to have the members express their opinions without registering an official vote to decide the issue. However, it is difficult to explain to a congregation that a straw vote is not final. Some members will invariably consider this vote to be their final and official opinion regardless of the way the total vote might go. It is also true that a straw vote is usually taken before the members have been fully informed on the meaning of the question of the future ministry of the church. The opinion vote or straw vote then becomes an emotional response rather than an informed determination.

The committee that made the plans for the Broadlands voting sought to be perfectly fair to the total community and used the opportunity of the straw vote to allow nonmembers to register their opinions. This is a noble concern, but the members are the ones who must make a consolidation effective. Since the decision was made that the official vote would be taken regardless of the outcome of the straw vote—and that both votes would be taken on the same day—the straw vote would have little consequence in the final decision.

This plan indicates the fair attitude of the committee and the cohesive relationship of the congregations in Broadlands. It cannot be assumed, however, that this procedure would work in every community. The sharing of information should always precede any voting. The giving of this information may be done in several ways:

1. A duplicate letter with full information on the proposal should be sent to every member of the churches involved.
2. Separate congregational meetings at which are present persons of responsible leadership to answer individual questions should be conducted.
3. Joint congregational meetings to share information across denominational lines are also suggested.

Under any circumstance the congregations should receive information on the proposed consolidation and be permitted to raise their questions at least two weeks before they are asked to vote. The members of each congregation involved should receive identical information. When it is taken, the vote should be the official expression of the will of the people.

The agenda for the voting meeting of the Broadlands congregations was outlined by the committee as follows:

1. Opening devotions and a hymn
2. A summary of the discussions and procedures to date
3. The individual voting of the congregations
4. Closing prayer and a hymn

There was agreement to make available absentee ballots to members unable to be present for the meeting up to and including the day of the joint congregational meeting (March 4, 1965). Nonresident and shut-in members would receive a letter explaining the background of the discussions along with a copy of the recommendations for uniting Broadlands churches (plan of union), which had been prepared by the steering committee. This mailing was scheduled for February 8, 1965.

A discussion of the recommendations resulted in two amendments by the steering committee. Under Condition 3: Property, it was agreed to remove paragraph B, which stated:

That the present United Church of Christ parsonage serve as the parsonage for the new union; that the present Methodist church building serve as the sanctuary and worship center for the new union; and that the present Methodist parsonage serve as facilities for Christian education (and other designated activities) for the new union.

Paragraph C was amended to read as follows:

That the new church union designate its own procedure for use of present buildings and disposal of property.

The three pastors were instructed to prepare the wording for the ballots to be used in voting.

A Decision Is Reached

The members of the three congregations gathered together in the Broadlands High School on March 4, 1965, to consider a crucial question regarding their future. The decision would be made on whether each congregation would continue its separate witness or whether each would agree to unite its efforts in one ministry.

Following the opening devotions and the singing of one of the great hymns of the church, a résumé of the discussions leading up to this meeting was given. Ample opportunity was given for questions and answers in order that everyone might be thoroughly informed. The plan of union was again presented and discussed, especially noting the amendments that the steering committee had suggested.

The members of the congregations would not be voting on denominational affiliation, but only on consolidation of the three congregations. The question of denominational affiliation would be answered at a later date and, as the people were informed, the assistance of the Commission on Church Planning and Development of the Illinois Council of Churches would be requested in this determination.

The denominational executives called for their respective congregations to meet separately for the purpose of raising questions and voting. Following the discussion period each denominational executive called upon the members of his respective congregation for a straw vote on the question of consolidation. Although the results of the straw vote were not made known, the executives were satisfied with the interest the vote revealed.

The official ballots were distributed in each congregation and the members voted. The steering committee had recommended that a two-thirds majority affirmative vote in each congregation would be necessary to effect the consolidation. Again the actual results of the vote were not made known. It was determined, however, that both the Methodist and the United Church of Christ congregations had more than the required two-thirds majority. The Evangelical United Brethren congregation's result was reported as one vote short of a two-thirds majority.

The congregations met again in joint session following the individual meetings. When the report was given that the Evangelical United Brethren congregation was one vote short of the required two-thirds majority, the congregation was urged to reconsider its vote. The members agreed to do so.

Following the closing prayer and the singing of a hymn, the meeting was brought to a close.

The number of votes necessary to approve the consolidation as determined by the steering committee was unusually high. The fact that there was little difficulty in obtaining this high percentage again attests to the excellent spirit of the people of Broadlands. Legally, it is not necessary to change local church constitutional provisions regarding voting, even on the question of consolidation. Few congregations require a two-thirds majority vote for passing resolutions. In the absence of a local church constitution, the constitution of the parent body of the congregation (denomination) should be followed.

In some states a legal vote of a congregation may be determined by the nonprofit corporation laws of the state. The requirement for voting under these laws calls for a simple majority vote. A committee working toward a consolidation should consult a local attorney before announcing the voting requirements when these are not determined by local constitutions.

The fact that the Evangelical United Brethren congregation was one vote short of the determined majority necessary to approve consolidation, and the added fact that the congregation had agreed to reconsider its vote, raised a question of the legality of the reconsideration. The legality of the matter was raised since the plan of union had not provided for a revote and the people were not informed that this might happen. The steering committee met on March 10, 1965, and agreed that the pastors should contact the denominational executives for a ruling on the matter.

The pastors received a report from each executive and, in late March, wrote a joint letter to all the members reporting the decisions of the executives. The letter stated that since there was no question regarding the decision of the members of the Methodist and the United Church of Christ congregations, both the Methodist district superintendent and the United Church of Christ conference minister agreed that the ruling decision should be made by the district superintendent of the Evangelical United Brethren church. The decision of the district superintendent was quoted in the letter to the members. The superintendent agreed:

> The Evangelical United Brethren congregation's action of "reconsideration," being a household matter with them, was unquestionably in order, and thus legal and binding. . . . Since no opposition had been raised by the Evangelical United Brethren members to him or to the pastor, and that no request had been made for revote, he concluded the "reconsideration" of March 4, as satisfactory agreement for Evangelical United Brethren participation in the [consolidation].

This decision meant that the vote of all three congregations on March 4 was valid; the consolidation had become a reality.

Several important matters remained to be decided, such as recommending the denominational affiliation, selecting a name for the congregation, setting a date for Charter Sunday, adopting a budget, planning for the organization of the congregation, and agreeing on the use of property. The steering committee moved ahead in planning recommendations on these matters.

A Denomination Is Chosen

A delegation from the steering committee, representing each congregation, met with the Commission on Church Planning and Development of the Illinois Council of Churches at the council offices in Springfield, Illinois. The delegation informed the commission of the procedure that led to the voting of the congregations on consolidation. They reported that the votes had been in the affirmative in all three congregations and hence asked for assistance from the commission in the determination of denominational affiliation. The delegation indicated that the particular denominational affiliation was not a real issue in the community.

The Commission on Church Planning and Development met on April 23, 1965, and reviewed the action of the three congregations in Broadlands and their request for assistance in the determination of denominational affiliation. After considerable deliberation a decision was reached and the recommendation was given to the denominational executives who had counseled with the three congregations during the negotiations. The executives met with the three congregations in joint session on April 25, 1965, and reported that the impartial recommendation of the Commission on Church Planning and Development was for the newly consolidated congregation to be affiliated with the Methodist denomination.

Although there were some persons in the community who were not completely satisfied with this recommendation, it was generally accepted by the people. Thus another major step toward complete unity had been achieved.

The steering committee met on May 11, 1965, to proceed with the final steps necessary to bring the new congregation into being. It was agreed that June 13 should be designated as Charter Sunday, at which time the members of the three congregations would accept the discipline of the Methodist denomination through complete affiliation. Each person would bring into this union a rich heritage from his past experience.

A nominating committee, including the three pastors and two representatives of each congregation, was appointed. This committee was assigned the task of nominating persons, assuring equal representation from each congregation, whose names would be presented to the new congregation for election to the following offices:

Trustees	(total 3)
Elders or stewards	(total 6)
Evangelism committee	(total 3)
Christian education committee	(total 3)
Stewardship committee	(total 3)
Finance committee	(total 3)

It was agreed that the chairman of the official council, the church school superintendent, the church treasurer, the financial secretary, and the lay delegates should be appointed from among the 21 elected officials.

The name of the new church was discussed. It was agreed that two names should be presented to each of the three congregations for consideration and that a final decision on the name would be made at the charter meeting on June 13. The suggested names were: Christ United Church and United Community Church.

The steering committee on consolidation met again on June 4, 1965, for its final session before the organization of the new congregation. A letter from the Methodist district superintendent giving information on the appointment of a new pastor to the congregation was read. It was agreed to invite the newly appointed pastor to the charter service of the congregation on June 13, and also to invite him to meet with the official council following the service.

The Methodist and Evangelical United Brethren pastors, who had worked so faithfully through the negotiation proceedings, had received other appointments from their denominations and would soon be leaving Broadlands to take up their work in these areas. Because of a prior commitment, the newly appointed pastor could not assume his new duties until August 1, 1965. The United Church of Christ pastor had received a call to another parish, but would not begin work there until August 1. The steering committee agreed that the United Church of Christ pastor would serve the consolidated church until August 1.

The nominating committee reported that it had been successful in its search for a slate of officers for the official council of the new church. The nominations were accepted by the steering committee and were to be presented to the congregations for election.

In a remarkably short length of time, the negotiations for the consolidation of the Methodist, Evangelical United Brethren, and United Church of Christ congregations of Broadlands, Illinois, were brought to a close. On June 13, 1965, a new congregation, affiliated with the Methodist denomination, was born. Every member of the former congregations—with the exception of one family of the United Church of Christ congregation who transferred to a church in another community prior to the organizational date—reaffirmed his loyalty to Christ by becoming a member of this new congregation. In all,

228 members were recorded on the new church roll in Broadlands that day.

Following an inspirational worship service, during which the names of all the members were announced, the new congregation met to conduct its first official business. Four names for the new congregation were given consideration. Two of these—Christ United Church and United Community Church —had been suggested by the steering committee. Two others— St. John's and St. John's United—were suggested from the floor at the time of the meeting. Of these four, United Community Church was accepted by the congregation. The slate of officers for the official council was elected. A six-month operational budget was approved.

Other matters considered and approved by the congregation included the following:

1. The present Methodist sanctuary would be used as the sanctuary and worship center for the new congregation.
2. The present United Church of Christ parsonage would be used as the parsonage for the new pastor.
3. The present Methodist parsonage would be used as an educational center (parish house for Christian education) on an experimental basis.
4. All church furniture and furnishings not used would be put in storage until needed or until disposed of.

Once again a demonstration of Christian love and concern resulted in unity of purpose for one segment of the church of Christ. Whatever adjustments may have been considered by the people of Broadlands, they chose consolidation as the most adequate solution to their problems. Through the concern of denominational leaders and representatives of the Illinois State Council of Churches, the people were supported and encouraged in their desire to become one congregation. It is this kind of united effort that will aid people in their search for solutions to the problems faced by the congregations in the town and country areas of America today.

Chapter Five

✝

Red Lodge Community Church United Church of Christ Red Lodge, Montana

RED LODGE, MONTANA, had its beginnings as a community in the late 1870's as a mining town. The abundant supply of coal and the quick market—supplying fuel for the steam locomotives of the Northern Pacific Railroad—brought a population of over 5,000 to the community by the early 1900's. There were another 2,000 to 3,000 people living near Red Lodge in the two other mining communities of Bearcreek and Washoe. Red Lodge became the county seat of Carbon County (population 8,000) and ultimately the shopping center for the surrounding area, remaining this today even though the population has declined to about 2,100 people in Red Lodge itself, and 30 to 40 people in the nearby communities of Bearcreek and Washoe. A mine disaster in 1943, the mechanization of mining operations, and the changeover to diesel locomotives by the Northern Pacific Railroad have resulted in the closing of all mines in the community, except one small operation that continues to produce a small amount of coal. Between 1950 and 1965, Red Lodge's population declined by 500. The beauty and natural resources of the area are presently being developed for leisure recreation opportunities. This will probably not cause a large increase in permanent population, but the service business to vacationers will increase employment opportunities.

The religious life of the community has been served by one Roman Catholic and six Protestant churches. The number of members in each church being small (Methodist 134; Congregational [United Church of Christ] 160; American Lutheran 150; Episcopalian 28; Assembly of God 25; Church of Christ 40; and Roman Catholic 600), effective programming was difficult. With the prospects of a further decline in population, there was certainly the possibility of a proportionate decline in church membership. The Methodist congregation was in an even more difficult situation, since it was part of a three-church parish consisting of the Red Lodge Methodist Church, the Luther Methodist Church of Luther, Montana, and the Roberts Methodist Church of Roberts, Montana.

In 1919 the members of the Methodist and Congregational churches in Red Lodge discussed the possibility of consolidation, so that they could provide a more effective ministry in the community. Even then there was competition among the churches and some serious-thinking people felt that something should be done. These discussions ended, not with a plan for consolidation, but with a determination to continue separate ministries in the community. Three other attempts toward achieving unity were made by these two congregations in the ensuing years, but these also failed. Reasons cited for these failures pointed to the fact that one congregation issued the invitation to discuss the possibility of consolidation to the other congregation. This indicated that the research and prompting of discussions had not been mutually acceptable before the discussions began. A second reason—given in retrospect—indicated that there had been a clash of personalities, which might have resulted from the fact that one congregation had played a major role in initiating the discussions. It was also noted that in each of the previous attempts one of the congregations was without ministerial leadership, which meant (or was imagined to result in) an imbalance in the negotiation leadership.

When one congregation in a community recognizes the need for an adjustment of the congregational units in order to improve the church program and strength, the natural impulse of some members is to issue an invitation to the members of a compatible congregation in the community to join them in a united church. Such an invitation tends to repulse those to whom it is given, since it precludes a discussion on denominational affiliation. When there is a need for interdenominational consideration of the church relationship in any community, which may be recognized first by one congregation, an invitation may be extended to other congregations, but it should be worded so that the intent of the congregation cannot be misconstrued. It should be an invitation to discuss the future of the church without a determination in the wording on what that future might be. Such an invitation should assume that the congregation issuing the invitation would be willing to lose its identity for the sake of a better ministry.

Sometimes the elements of nature play a role in leading churches to make decisions about their future. In the spring of 1963 the back basement wall of the Congregational (UCC) church caved in due to heavy rains. A representative of the Church Buildings Department, United Church Board for Homeland Ministries, encouraged the congregation to evaluate its witness in the community in the face of a declining population and an overchurched situation. The study was completed by late fall and the results of the study convinced many members in leadership positions that they should again initiate exploratory discussions with the Methodist congregation regarding the future of these two churches. Judicatory representatives of each denomination were contacted and they agreed to assist the congregations in these new discussions. Consequently, a unity committee, composed of representatives from both congregations, was appointed and the first meeting was scheduled. The Methodist district superintendent and the Congregational (UCC) conference minister agreed to attend this meeting.

The Beginning of Discussions

The unity committee met on January 12, 1964, and considered the possibility of starting conversations on the matter of consolidation. Both the Methodist district superintendent and the Congregational (UCC) conference minister were present for this meeting and discouraged the idea of forming a federated church. They suggested that the committee explore the possibility of joining the two congregations into a community church with a denominational affiliation. It was noted that there were 161 community churches with denominational affiliation already in existence in the state of Montana. The committee was informed that a nondenominational community church faces difficulty in obtaining pastors, in matters of mission, church school curriculum, record keeping, and other important work. If the congregations wanted to become a community church, the committee was told that they could choose affiliation with either of the two denominations represented or choose affiliation with a third denomination.

The first task would be to determine the feasibility of congregational consolidation; if acceptable, the choice of denominational affiliation could then be made. So that decisions and plans could be made intelligently, with as little bias as possible, a program of study of the Methodist and Congregational (UCC) denominations regarding polity, organizations, lay groups, property, program, and missions was inaugurated by the committee. The denominational executives assured the committee that the two present ministers could continue to serve their congregations until a consolidation could be effected. At that time the congregation could select a minister from the denomination to which it would be affiliated.

The consolidation of two congregations in any community requires much work. It cannot be achieved overnight and does not come without painful and difficult decisions. The sentimental attachment to buildings, which some people possess, must be gently discouraged. The goal must be to create a more effective religious witness in the community rather than to perpetuate a particular denominational influence. The people of the congregations must be convinced of the need for such an adjustment and realize that agreement across denominational lines is not necessarily as new as it might seem. Congregational consolidation in the years of the great depression was not unusual. Interdenominational agreements to work closely together in the locating of churches to avoid competition is now commonplace in most areas of the country. The Presbyterian and Congregational denominations in Montana agreed in 1919 not to start competing congregations in communities of less than 10,000 population. All these factors helped to convince the members of the committee that they should proceed with the discussions on consolidation.

As evidence of their own conviction, members of the unity committee, meeting on January 19, 1964, adopted the following recommendation:

The combined committees of the Red Lodge Methodist and Congregational (UCC) Churches go on record as recommending that we become one church.

In order that the congregations might consider and vote on this recommendation, special congregational meetings were scheduled for February 2, 1964. The Congregational (UCC) pastor agreed to prepare a letter to be sent to every home of both congregations to explain the recommendation and announce the congregational meetings.

In compliance with the earlier decision of the committee to study each denomination, the pastor of the Methodist church gave a brief history of the Methodist movement. Following a discussion of this presentation, it was agreed to invite the synod executive of the Presbytery of Yellowstone, Synod of the Rockies, United Presbyterian Church in the U.S.A., to speak to the committee about the history, government, and beliefs of the Presbyterian church. When it came time to choose a denominational affiliation the committee felt that there might be an advantage in selecting a denomination other than the two represented; knowledge of the Presbyterian church would be helpful.

The synod executive of the Yellowstone Presbytery prepared a written report that related the history of interdenominational cooperation in the state of Montana. This report was discussed by the committee when it met on January 26, 1964. The report showed that, as a result of a meeting on July 8, 1919, in Miles City, Montana, the Congregational, Methodist, and Presbyterian churches agreed not to compete with each other in small communities. The mechanics of the agreement have been carried out through the assistance of the Montana Council of Churches and have resulted in many adjustments of congregations that have chosen to become community churches affiliated with one of the agreeing denominations. By 1963 the state of Montana had 82 communities that were committed to Methodist oversight, 31 committed to Congregational (UCC), and 46 to Presbyterian. In each adjustment resulting in a community church, the members of the two remaining denominational groups became members of the resultant congregation regardless of the denominational affiliation. The Baptist and Christian denominations, as well as others, participate in these cooperative efforts.

In further consideration of the local situation and the pending meetings of the congregations to vote on a recommendation to consolidate, the committee formulated the following statements regarding their reasons for the recommendation:

1. It was Jesus' intent that his followers be one—"Holy Father, keep them in thy name which thou hast given me, that they may be one, even as we are one" (John 17:11).
2. While our congregations are united in community efforts six days a week, our churches tend to divide us on Sunday, contrary to the main purpose of our religion.
3. Consolidation would increase the total Protestant Christian witness in the community.
4. Overhead expenses are increasing in both churches.
5. There is a decrease in population in the local community.
6. There are recommendations from national and state levels toward union.
7. Both churches are facing major building needs.
8. Both congregations are compatible.
9. It would eliminate duplication of work.
10. There is a decreasing number of available personnel.
11. There is a long-range shortage of ministers.
12. There is a close similarity in theological beliefs and practices.

It was agreed that these reasons would be given and explained to both congregations at their separate meetings on February 2, 1964.

A Decision Is Made

The meetings of the two congregations were conducted in their respective churches following the morning worship services on the first Sunday in February. The congregations acted upon the recommendation of the unity committee; namely, that the Methodist and Congregational (UCC) congregations of Red Lodge, Montana, unite. The reasons for the recommendation as prepared by the committee were given and discussed. The recommendation did not include a suggestion about denominational affiliation; however, the people were informed that they would have an opportunity to decide this at a later date. The results of the voting, made known to the congregations before the meetings were closed, were as follows:

	Yes	*No*	*Abstaining*
Congregational (UCC)	40	6	1
Methodist	50	1	0

Both congregations were overwhelmingly in favor of the consolidation; the unity committee had its directive to move ahead to work out the details.

It is unusual for congregations to vote on consolidation with such a majority in the affirmative without some idea of what their future denominational affiliation will be. In the past few years congregations of other communities have voted on similar motions of consolidation with the understanding that the affiliation of the resultant congregation would be decided later. In several of these communities the motion was rejected because the people were not inclined to vote for unity without knowing their future denominational identity. One might suspect that these congregations were not really interested in unity; however, once the suggestion for denominational affiliation was made, and a revote taken, some of these congregations approved it without difficulty and achieved consolidation. The action of the Red Lodge churches proves the confidence of the people in the unity committee and further proves that their concern for a stronger program was greater than their loyalty to a particular denomination. The mood and the motives of these people were right for this vote.

When the committee met in the evening of the day of voting, they began to determine ways of bringing the two congregations into a closer working unit before the actual consolidation. A merger of the youth groups was discussed, but it was agreed that they should not be united until the fall of 1964, when a new series of programs would begin. Joint worship services for the congregations were planned for the lenten season. The two pastors were asked to work out a new order of worship for these services and to arrange for a mutually acceptable time schedule for them. The loose offerings received in the joint services would be divided equally between the two congregations. Each congregation would provide an equal number of ushers for each service. The services on February 16 and 23 would be conducted in the Congregational (UCC) church and those on March 1 and 8 would be conducted in the Methodist church. The combined choirs would be asked to sing at each of these services.

There was a felt need for a joint building and grounds committee; the trustees of each congregation were designated as members of this committee. They were asked to inspect all the property, including the condition of the heating plants, in relation to present structural conditions, and to note the adequacy of facilities for a pastor's study and of kitchen equipment.

The building committee met with the unity committee on February 16, 1964. A chairman and secretary of the building committee were appointed. An inspection of the property of both congregations was scheduled for February 19, 1964.

The unity committee agreed that the official board of the Methodist congregation should meet with the board of deacons and deaconesses of the Congregational (UCC) church to plan for a joint Easter service.

The pastor of the Congregational (UCC) church gave a report on the history, polity, and beliefs of the Congregational denomination and its ultimate consolidation with the Evangelical and Reformed denomination to form the United Church of Christ. This report was discussed at some length, which enabled the members of the committee to understand better the difference between the Methodist and the United Church of Christ denominations.

The building committee began its work on February 19, 1964, by discussing the building and equipment needs of a consolidated congregation. Since Christian education was considered to be of prime importance, representatives of the Christian education committees of each congregation were asked to meet with the building committee so that their concerns could be expressed. A local building contractor, who was also a member of the Methodist congregation, was co-opted by the committee to inspect the two properties with them and make professional recommendations for possible alterations or additions.

A member of the building committee was appointed to obtain information from the courthouse on the size of lots owned by the two congregations as well as the extent of the several lots adjoining the Methodist property, but not owned by them.

When the building committee met again on February 23, 1964, a thorough inspection of the Methodist and Congregational (UCC) church buildings was made. While the men observed the structural fitness of the two buildings, the women members discussed the future needs of the church school.

After the inspection was over it was determined that the

Methodist church building was in much better structural condition than the Congregational (UCC) church. To satisfy the needs of a combined church school, which the women reported would require seven additional rooms, the building committee agreed that the best procedure would be to erect a two-story educational unit on the rear of the Methodist church. The contractor, present at this meeting, agreed to prepare an estimate of the cost of such a building.

A plan to bring the two church schools together immediately was developed by the women members in their separate session. The plan suggested that the nursery, kindergarten, first, second, fifth, and sixth grades begin sessions together in the Methodist church and that the third, fourth, seventh, eighth, and senior high classes meet in the Congregational (UCC) church. The shortage of church school staff members and the availability of space were cited as reasons for taking this immediate step. The plan was scheduled to be presented for approval of the unity committee before the change would take place.

The report of the building committee, including the recommendation that the Methodist church building be used by the consolidated congregation, was presented to the unity committee. The possibility of erecting a two-story educational unit for Christian education was mentioned, and the following recommendation on alterations to the present Methodist church were made:

> Omit one front stairway, and possibly by recessing the wall behind the altar, make room for a choir loft. The heating system should be reconditioned.

An estimate of the cost of these renovations was promised. It was further suggested that the Methodist church could be used for worship and that the Congregational (UCC) church could be used for church school until the building or renovations would be completed.

The contractor reported that alterations to the Congregational (UCC) church, necessary to meet the needs of a consolidated congregation, would be too expensive. It was his opinion that the Congregational (UCC) property was salable while the Methodist property was not.

The suggested plan for combining the church schools imme-

diately was approved, and arrangements were made to send a
letter to the parents of all church school pupils notifying them
of the change.

An overnight retreat for the two youth groups on March 6–7
resulted in a vote to unite the two groups into one. Twenty-
one young people and four adult leaders participated in the
retreat.

The Problem of Denominational Affiliation

The synod executive of the Presbytery of Yellowstone met
with the unity committee on March 8, 1964. In his presentation he retraced the history of cooperation among the Protestant denominations in the state of Montana, as reflected in the
paper he had made available to the committee at its meeting
on January 26, 1964. Much of this information was the result
of a thorough discussion of the initial paper. The synod executive ,also spoke of the history, polity, and beliefs of the Presbyterian denomination.

In the ensuing discussion, the executive showed the committee a plaque setting forth community denominational cooperation in Montana, and indicated that such a plaque was displayed in the narthex of the 159 community churches that had
a denominational affiliation in Montana. Furthermore, it was
expected that several other churches would be displaying such
a plaque before the end of the year.

The synod executive expressed the hope that a consolidation—if one would be consummated in Red Lodge—could
come on the 45th anniversary of the first historical ecumenical meeting in Montana conducted on July 8, 1919. He also
encouraged the group to choose a denominational affiliation
and organic union rather than develop a federated relationship, because a federation is too cumbersome for one minister
to handle. He indicated on a map the location of the denominationally affiliated community churches in Montana. It was
clear to the committee that they should consider affiliation
with either the Methodist denomination or the Congregational (UCC), rather than the Presbyterian denomination. If
the congregation would affiliate with the Presbyterian denomination it would be geographically cut off from other congregations of this denomination.

The committee was encouraged to arrive at a recommendation of its own regarding denominational affiliation. If the

committee would be unable to agree on such a recommendation, the Planning and Strategy Committee of the Montana Council of Churches could be asked for advice and assistance.

The committee, after discussing the presentation and suggestions of the Presbyterian synod executive, agreed that it would be able to arrive at a recommendation on the denominational affiliation of the church within the next two meetings and that this recommendation could be given to the congregations for vote early in April.

It was also agreed that the people should think in terms of erecting a new church building rather than trying to renovate or add to either of the present structures. Church attendance at the time indicated that the present facilities may prove to be too small. Also, by erecting a new edifice, the ideas of "my church" and "your church" would be replaced by the thought of "our church." The cost of a new church was estimated at $75,000.

The building committee met on March 11, 1964, to consider the costs of various proposals that had been made for renovations and new construction. A heating and plumbing contractor, a building contractor, and an architect who had been consulted gave estimates of costs for the following proposals:

1. New construction costs would be approximately $17 to $19 per square foot.
2. A two-story, eight-room addition to the Methodist building would cost approximately $19,000.
3. Plumbing and heating renovations were estimated at $3,000. The plumbing and heating costs, plus the addition to the Methodist building, would amount to approximately $22,000.
4. The estimated cost of a new building with adequate church school facilities was given at $50,000.

The building committee agreed that the consolidated congregation would have three alternatives regarding its building needs.

1. Remodel the Methodist church building.
2. Construct an addition of one or two stories to the Methodist church for church school use.
3. Build a new church on the present site of the Congregational (UCC) church and parsonage.

It was reported that the Methodist building was in better condition and should be used if a remodeling program is undertaken, but the Congregational (UCC) property would offer the best location for new construction.

The committee agreed to present the building alternatives to the unity committee for further consideration and for possible recommendation to the congregations.

The committee further expressed the opinion that a decision on denominational affiliation should be made before any changes are made in the property. Recognizing that this was not in its area of responsibility, the committee nevertheless unanimously agreed to recommend to the unity committee that the two congregations consolidate and become affiliated with the United Church of Christ.

When the unity committee met on March 15, 1964, the report of the building committee was the first consideration. This report included the following observations:

> It is the opinion of this committee that if we should plan to remodel one of the present church buildings, the Methodist church building should be used, as it is now in the better condition and offers the best possibilities. Proposed remodeling of this building with the addition of a two-story, 45' x 50', eight-room educational wing in the rear, would cost approximately $23,000. For new construction, the committee recommends using the Congregational (UCC) property.

After full discussion, the committee agreed that a decision on the matter of buildings could not be reached until the consolidation had been effected and the denominational affiliation determined.

Ministerial leadership for the proposed consolidated congregation was discussed. It was noted that the congregations would have difficulty in getting pastors if each continued its separate witness, but combined, the resultant congregation would have little difficulty in obtaining the leadership needed. The problem of ministerial leadership for the other two congregations in the Methodist parish came under discussion. It was generally believed that the Luther Methodist congregation might be encouraged to come to the Red Lodge Community Church. It was agreed, however, that the Red Lodge Church after consolidation should continue to furnish ministerial leadership to the Roberts congregation as long as the two ministers were in residence, regardless of the denominational affiliation chosen. The community would probably need the services of both pastors for at least one year, and possibly two. It was noted, however, that when all details of the consolidation have been worked out and the congregation served by one pastor, this pastor would be too busy in Red Lodge to serve also the Roberts congregation. Perhaps the Roberts congregation would then be able to make other pastoral arrangements. The committee agreed to meet with representatives of both the Luther and Roberts congregations to discuss these matters with them.

A poll of the nine voting members of the committee was taken to determine their preference regarding a recommendation on denominational affiliation. Eight members indicated a desire to recommend affiliation with the United Church of Christ denomination and one preferred the Methodist denomination. The eight who favored a recommendation for the United Church of Christ gave the following reasons, among others, for their choice.

1. The United Church of Christ is already representative of several uniting denominational groups.
2. One effort of this denomination is the reuniting of the Body of Christ—the church.
3. The denominational name of the United Church of Christ signifies unity. Dispensing with both the Congregational and Methodist names, by which the congregations are known in the community, would represent a compromise, and the people could more readily accept the thought of "our church."
4. Becoming a part of the United Church of Christ would bring an end to unfounded fears of members of both congregations that the Methodist system of pastor placement could mean a change in pastors at any time.
5. Fewer Methodists than Congregationalists were strongly opposed to consolidation.
6. Congregationalist (UCC) members would find it difficult to renounce their tradition of freedom of the local church.

The committee member favoring Methodist affiliation had no personal objections to a recommendation that the consolidated church become a part of the United Church of Christ, but felt a strong obligation to support the Methodist side for the sake of the Roberts Methodist Church.

Since three committee members were absent, it was agreed that the committee would vote on a recommendation of denominational affiliation to submit to the congregations at the next meeting. The congregations would be asked to meet separately following the worship service on April 12, 1964, to vote on the denominational affiliation. The two pastors and the secretary of each congregation agreed to compose a letter to be sent to the members of both congregations announcing the recommendation of the unity committee and the date of the congregational meetings. The hope was expressed that officers of the new community church could be elected by the first of June.

The final plans for the meeting of the congregations were made on March 22, 1964. If the congregations vote favorably on the recommendation of denominational affiliation, the unity committee agreed that the actual consolidation would take place on July 8, 1964, serving thus as a statewide celebration of the forty-fifth anniversary of the beginning of interdenominational cooperation in the state of Montana.

The official recommendation on denominational affiliation, which the committee acted upon, was that the committee go on record as recommending to the congregations that the two churches become the Red Lodge Community Church, affiliated with the United Church of Christ. Three members of the committee were absent from the meeting, but each was polled by telephone for his vote on the question. When all votes were in, the tabulation revealed eleven votes in the affirmative and one negative.

The question was raised as to whether the other two congregations in the Methodist parish were entitled to vote on the recommendation as members of the Methodist congregation. The Methodist pastor was asked to check with the Methodist district superintendent on this, asking also for a letter from him verifying a former statement he had made—that the Methodist conference would permit the pastor to remain with the united church for at least one year.

It was agreed that the two pastors and the secretaries of the congregations would meet the following week to compose a letter to the congregations explaining the recommendation of the unity committee regarding affiliation. It was further agreed:

1. Ballots would be enclosed with the letters to the congregations.
2. Persons who could not be present for the congregational

meetings on April 12, could vote *in absentia* on the ballots enclosed in the letters.

3. All ballots would have to be signed to be valid.
4. All absentee ballots would have to be returned by 1 P.M. on April 12, 1964.
5. If a family with several voting members should not receive enough copies of the ballots, the ballot could be copied and would be accepted if properly signed and received on time.

It was suggested that the youth fellowship have a coffee hour for all members who desired to stay for a report on the balloting following the morning worship service on April 12. The votes would be counted by the unity committee and announced after 1 P.M.

If the vote on the denominational affiliation would be in the negative, the committee agreed that the previous vote of the congregations to unite would stand and that a new committee would be appointed to attempt another affiliation agreement. If the vote would be in the affirmative, it was agreed that the officers of both congregations would terminate their offices and the pastors would appoint a nominating committee to propose a slate of officers for the community church to serve until the end of the year.

The committee approved a motion that the present pastors should continue to serve the congregation for a period of at least one year. It was understood that this would depend on an affirmative vote for the consolidation and approval of the conferences.

The parish relationship of the Methodist congregation was a continuing concern of the committee, especially as that church related to the Roberts congregation. A meeting with the official board of the Roberts congregation was scheduled for April 2. The procedure and expectations of the Red Lodge consolidation could be fully explained at this time.

Immediately following the joint worship service on April 12, 1964, the two congregations met separately to conduct the business of the specially called congregational meetings. Notices of the meetings had been given in a letter to all the members, as well as being announced on two successive Sundays in the church bulletin. The purpose of the meetings was to vote on the recommendation of the unity committee, that the Red Lodge Methodist Church and the Red Lodge Congregational (UCC) Church become the Red Lodge Community

Church, affiliated with the United Church of Christ. Following discussion of the recommendation a vote was taken in each congregation according to its own procedure.

When the tabulation was completed, the following results were reported:

	Yes	No	Total
Congregational (UCC)	44	0	44
Methodist	29	1	30
Total Votes			74

A New Congregation Is Formed

Immediately following the report of the voting, a special meeting of the new congregation to be organized and known as the Red Lodge Community Church, United Church of Christ, was called for the purpose of conducting business of immediate necessity.

1. Two delegates were elected to represent the congregation at the United Church of Christ state conference at Miles City, Montana, on April 29–May 1, 1964. The pastors were authorized to appoint a third representative at a later time.
2. It was agreed that the official boards of the former Methodist and Congregational (UCC) congregations should meet on April 15, to select for the new congregation a slate of officers who would serve until an election could be conducted at the annual meeting of the congregation in January, 1965.
3. The suggestion of planning a special service commemorating the 45th anniversary of the ecumenical meeting conducted in Miles City in 1919 and the formal organization of the Red Lodge Community Church was discussed. It was agreed to refer this matter to the new church officers after their appointment.

Three days later, on April 15, 1964, the officers met to begin the task of uniting the two congregations as directed by the congregations in their votes of April 12. Several matters brought to the attention of the officers were decided without difficulty. It was agreed that the women's organizations would meet separately for their next meetings to allow the Methodist group to take care of some unfinished items.

The name Red Lodge Community Church would be used in all future newspaper articles and radio broadcasts. A new roadway sign was authorized and new stationery ordered, each of which would note the new church name. It was agreed also that the congregations would operate under separate budgets until the end of the Methodist church year on May 31. Other items of business included the following:

1. A constitution committee was appointed.
2. It was agreed to have the building and grounds committee, which was appointed by the unity committee, continue to serve.
3. It was agreed that all services after April 19, 1964, would be conducted in the Methodist building.
4. A nominating committee was appointed to select a slate of officers for the new congregation. It was agreed that the following offices would be filled: moderator and vice-moderator, six trustees, five deacons and five deaconesses, three members of a Christian education committee, church clerk, treasurer, music committee chairman, church school superintendent and assistant superintendent, and an auditing committee.

   It was agreed that these officers would be elected without specified terms, but it was understood that they would complete the calendar year. Officers with specified terms would be elected at the annual congregational meeting, which would be conducted in January, 1965.

   It was further agreed that the slate of officers, which would be prepared by the nominating committee, would be elected on May 17, and would take office on June 1.
5. The Christian education committee reported that church school would be conducted on a weekday morning during the summer rather than Sunday morning. It was explained that it would be easier to secure teachers for this type of program. The sessions would be two hours in length.
6. The pastors were asked to develop an order of worship to be used by the congregations in the future.
7. October 25, 1964, was suggested as a possible date for a special service to recognize the organization of the Red Lodge Community Church and to commemorate the 45th anniversary of the beginning of ecumenical cooperation in Montana. A committee was appointed to make the necessary arrangements.
8. The church school superintendent and music committee (when elected) were authorized to place orders for needed materials when necessary. It was agreed to place an immediate order for 25 additional United Church of Christ hymnbooks.

Both pastors stressed the point that they considered themselves co-pastors of the newly created congregation, although it had not yet been officially organized. They indicated that all members should feel free to call upon either of them in time of need regardless of former affiliation.

The building committee, meeting on April 30, 1964, agreed that the congregation should not spend more money than necessary on any remodeling program at the present time. The opinion was expressed that a new building may be needed in a year or two, but should not be proposed immediately. The facilities being used for church school were considered to be adequate for the summer session and no change in the program was recommended. The committee did decide, however, to remove the furnishings from the Congregational (UCC) church building as soon as possible and to use as much of the equipment as possible to augment the furnishings in the Methodist building. After the furnishings were removed from the Congregational (UCC) church, the building might be rented for meetings, luncheons, and/or parties of various local organizations.

Since both congregations owned parsonages in Red Lodge, the building committee was faced with a decision on which parsonage would be used when only one pastor would be serving the consolidated congregation. The Methodist parsonage was in much better condition than the one owned by the Congregational (UCC) church and it was agreed that it should be used as the parsonage and that the Congregational (UCC) parsonage should be remodeled for the use of the church school. The committee further agreed to recommend to the officers to be elected on May 17 that the fellowship hall on the Congregational (UCC) church property be moved from its present location to the rear of the Methodist church building and that it be remodeled to accommodate five church school classes.

The first official meeting of the Red Lodge Community Church was conducted on June 7, 1964, following the regular morning worship service. The nominating committee presented a slate of officers, an equal number of persons being nominated from each congregation. The officers, as nominated, were elected to serve until the annual meeting of the congregation, which was scheduled for January 17, 1965. Future nominations would be made without regard to former church affiliation.

The congregations were encouraged to finish out the year 1964 by paying their benevolent monies to the Methodist and United Church of Christ denominations respectively. The youth of the Methodist church were encouraged to participate in the Methodist summer camp program for that year, since some of them were officers of the state organization.

The polity structure of a United Church of Christ congregation was adopted. A constitution committee was appointed to write a constitution that would follow the suggestions of the General Synod of that denomination.

The Red Lodge Community Church was inaugurated amid the prayers, hopes, and excitement of an entire community. After five attempts and four failures the community church moved ahead with confidence.

The formal dedication of the Red Lodge Community Church and the commemoration of the 45th anniversary of the "Every Community Service Endeavor" of Montana took place in Red Lodge on December 20, 1964. Officials of the United Church of Christ, Methodist, and Presbyterian denominations were on hand to congratulate the people of this community in their successful efforts to establish closer unity among church groups and to meet the challenge of a new day through organic union in the face of a declining population. Thus another congregation was permitted to receive and display the plaque of community churches of Montana that have denominational affiliation and that minister with open mind and heart to the Methodists, Presbyterians, Congregationalists (UCC), and others of the area.

Since the consummation of this consolidation, the congregation has continued to worship in the Methodist building, which has been slightly renovated to care for the expanded needs of the congregation. The Congregational (UCC) church building and parsonage have been sold to the Roman Catholic Church, which intends to use them for its educational program.

Study committees have been appointed by the congregation to consider every aspect of its witness in the community and to determine the building needs of the future. Red Lodge Community Church is moving ahead.

Even though the mining industry of the community no longer provides the employment opportunities and economical resources that are necessary for growth and stability, the people who have remained in Red Lodge are not discouraged. A new and exciting future seems to be developing for the community and for the community church as this part of Montana becomes more and more an area for leisure recreation activities. Red Lodge is a beautiful community, situated at the very entrance of Yellowstone National Park. As the people of America have more leisure time, many will undoubtedly find their way to this community, and the people of Red Lodge and the Red Lodge Community Church will greet them with a united effort unsurpassed in any community.

Chapter Six

✠

The Union Church

THE PAGES OF CHURCH history in America are filled with accounts of many forms and practices of cooperative efforts among the various denominations, which have been tried with varying degrees of success. Some of these attempts have brought about a closer unity of congregations, while others have ended in further separation. One heritage of more than two hundred years that has, in some cases, resulted in close cooperation between two denominations is known as the union church.

The union church had its beginning in America, in the state of Pennsylvania. It was started by Protestant Christians of the Lutheran and Reformed persuasions who came to this country from Germany. Being frugal people with a great love for the church and their native heritage, it was not unnatural for them to consider the possibilities of erecting one building in a community to house two congregations. They worked out a system whereby the Lutheran congregation had use of the facilities for worship services one Sunday and the Reformed (later the United Church of Christ) congregation, the next. It was not at all uncommon for some members to attend the services of both churches.

In the early days, ministers were scarce and most of them rode circuits of four to eight churches. With this demand on the leadership, it was not possible for every congregation to have services every Sunday. Those persons who belonged to a union church had the advantage of listening to sermons more often than others. The difference in the order of service and the theological orientation posed no problem at all, but rather offered a variety in the worship experience that could not be enjoyed in any other kind of church situation. A bonus for this variety came in the fact that one congregation was not responsible for paying for the services of the pastor who happened to be preaching for the other congregation on a given Sunday.

When the church school movement began to flourish, the union church members took to it readily. Here was a "natural" for ecumenical endeavors beyond the shared use of a building. Union church schools came into existence and members of both congregations met together for the study of the Scriptures. Many variations of the church school program were evidenced and often many types of literature were used. In most cases there was a deliberate attempt to have the union church school free and clear of any denominational attachment. It was important to some that the church school officers rotate each year so that the superintendent would be a Lutheran one year and a Reformed person the next. Many alternated the curriculum materials on the same basis. Such an arrangement often resulted in what some have called a third congregation.

Wherever the German people of the Lutheran and Reformed persuasions migrated, they usually organized a union church. Besides those in Pennsylvania, there are still in existence several union relationships in Maryland and one in North Carolina. Records show that many such unions once existed through the Shenandoah Valley of Virginia and other places.

The property—consisting of the church building and grounds, the cemetery, and often a sexton's home, pavilion, and several acres of land—was almost always owned jointly by the two congregations. Care and maintenance costs were shared on a fifty-fifty basis. This practice continues in most of the 163 union churches still in existence.

Almost as soon as the union church movement was started, some of the congregations began to move out of the relationship and build single-congregation churches. Many times the "moving-out congregation" did not move far from the old building. Many built on an adjoining lot, across the street, or on the next corner, and often constructed buildings in the same style as the union church structure. Some separations resulted in ill feelings between the members of the two congregations.

Although one might assume that the union church is an excellent example of ecumenical cooperation, this is not always true. The joint ownership of property may be the only thing the two congregations hold in common, and even this creates a magnitude of problems in some cases. The management of the property becomes difficult when one congregation feels strongly about a renovation program, an addition, or a needed repair and the other congregation does not recognize such need. Ecumenicity may cease to exist at this point. The use of facilities is also a point of disagreement at times. In some cases it is necessary to print a detailed schedule of worship services and organizational meetings to avoid confusion among the members. Congregational jealousies, disparity in membership, and the feeling of being dominated are other factors that prevent full harmony in many union churches.

In 1945 the synods of the two denominations organized the Commission on the Welfare of the Union Church for the purpose of assisting congregations in the union relationship to make necessary adjustments forced upon them by a changing society and/or their own internal difficulties. Consultants representing the two denominations began work as counselors for the congregations and have assisted many to achieve the kind of adjustment they have desired for more effective witness in their respective communities. Such adjustments have not always meant a separation of the joint relationship. At times it has been wiser to remain union and work out a schedule whereby each congregation can worship every Sunday. Sometimes a union church school is divided into two denominational schools. Sometimes the two congregations decide on a course of action leading to organic consolidation. Some adjustments can be agreed to in one meeting while other agreements take years to accomplish. The more drastic the necessary adjustment becomes, the longer it takes to accomplish it.

A complete understanding exists between the denominational consultants whose trust in one another cannot be questioned. Their friendship extends beyond the meeting room in a local church and enables them to develop strategy on a completely cooperative basis. Their intent of purpose, when called to assist a union church, is to lead the people in their own determination of what adjustment would be best for the total community. The particular denominational concern that they represent is a secondary consideration. Trust and understanding are essentials in any cooperative endeavor and must always be evident in the leadership. When those who are expected to provide guidance in an ecumenical discussion exemplify these essentials, the mood of the local people is similarly influenced. Such was the case in the two case studies that follow.

A
St. John's United Church of Christ
Laurys Station, Pennsylvania

Lehigh County, Pennsylvania, was far from being the industrial center it is today when the St. John's Union Church was organized in 1872. Farming was a major industry for the people in the little community of Laurys Station, which is situated at the northern edge of the county line at the foothills of the Pocono Mountains and approximately seven miles north of Allentown. The people were content with their uncomplicated way of life and the choice beauty of the surrounding landscape. Although they spoke English when they went to town, their native German language was the preferred means of communication in their home and in discussing the events of the day with their neighbors. Allentown was a growing city, but it was seven miles away, a long distance to travel in a wagon or buggy. The general store at Laurys Station offered all the necessities the people could want or afford. They took comfortable refuge in the isolation of their community.

When there was no church in Laurys Station, religious worship and teaching was basically a home program. The people gathered together in their homes for hymn sings and the reading of the Scriptures. The nearest church was in the community of Egypt, approximately three miles south of Laurys Station. There were two congregations in Egypt (Lutheran and Reformed), and both used the same building. When the weather permitted, some of the people at Laurys Station made the trip to Egypt to share in a formal service and to partake of Holy Communion. The distance, the slow mode of transportation, and the fact that the people at Laurys Station recognized the need for more religious training for their chil-

dren caused them to consider seriously the building of a
church in their own community.

Neighbors came together and discussed the needs of their
religious faith. They knew that almost all the residents were
members of either the Lutheran or the Reformed persuasion.
Beyond this there was a sense of unity that comes when people
share the same concerns, joys, sorrows, and hardships of a
close-knit community. Could the people at Laurys Station
erect one building to house two congregations representing
their religious preferences? Egypt had a union church and
there were many more scattered throughout Pennsylvania.
Finding no real objection to their thought, they decided that a
church would be built and that it would be union in order to
care for both the Lutheran and Reformed congregations. The
people were now determined to organize.

On May 12, 1872, in a simple but moving organizational
service, the congregational life of this community first took
form. For a name they chose St. John's Union Church of
Laurys Station. A building to house the activities of these two
congregations and to provide them with a central place of
worship was constructed that same year. This building stands
today and is still in use, symbolizing the determined faith of
its builders. Through several renovation projects and at least
one major addition, the facilities are completely adequate to
meet the needs of these people as they continue their service to
God through this church.

Since neither of the congregations at Laurys Station was
large enough to support their own pastor, it was necessary for
them to be yoked with other churches in the shared use of
pastors. Several church adjustments through the years finally
brought into being a three-church yoked arrangement constituted by the union churches at Egypt, Cementon, and Laurys
Station. A pastor served the three Lutheran congregations,
preaching in two of the congregations one Sunday and one the
next. The United Church of Christ pastor had much the same
schedule, alternating Sundays with the Lutheran pastor. Questions raised on a Sunday morning today in many union
churches were never considered by the members of St. John's.
Today one union church member may ask, "Is this the Lutheran Sunday or the United Church of Christ (Reformed)
Sunday?" What he really means is, "Will my preacher be in
church today or will their preacher be there?" The St. John's

people at Laurys Station would only ask, "Will there be a preaching service today?" The important thing for them was that services would be conducted.

The Beginning of Change

Nothing ever stays the same, even the harmonious relationship in a union church. Industry began to flourish in Lehigh County. People began to stop farming and take jobs in the steel mills and cement factories. The population increased in the area around Allentown, Egypt, and Cementon, but showed only minor growth at Laurys Station. The demands upon the church in the growth areas, especially at Egypt, caused the official boards of the two congregations in that union church to evaluate their program to determine if they were really meeting the needs of their people. Late in 1962 each congregation was still on a biweekly schedule of worship services, and the church school program was still union and overcrowding the facilities. The Lutheran council and the United Church of Christ consistory extended an invitation to the consultants for the Commission on the Welfare of the Union Church to meet with them to discuss their future. Primary concerns were to have worship services for both congregations every Sunday and to establish denominationally oriented church schools.

The council and the consistory, with the help of the consultants, developed a schedule of worship services and church school programs that met their approval. The proposed schedule for the Egypt congregations provided for a complete separation of program but continued use of the same facilities. This could be achieved with little confusion if one congregation used the sanctuary for worship services while the other congregation conducted its own church school program in the Christian education building. It was suggested that this schedule be maintained on a regular basis.

United Church of Christ		
Worship—	9:30 A.M.	—Lutheran Church School
United Church of Christ		
Church School—	10:45 A.M.	—Lutheran Worship

Since the suggested change in the Egypt program would affect the schedules of the other two union churches in the yoked relationship, it was agreed that a joint meeting of the councils and consistories of the entire parish should be conducted. On December 14, 1962, the official boards of the Egypt,

Cementon, and Laurys Station union churches met with the consultants to consider the proposed schedule changes for Cementon and Laurys Station necessitated by the request for increased services of the pastors by the Egypt congregations.

When the service schedules of all the congregations were reviewed it was noted that if the Egypt congregations made the suggested changes, the Cementon congregations would have to advance their hour of worship fifteen minutes, from 8:30 A.M. to 8:15 A.M. The change for Laurys Station was more drastic. The proposed schedule meant a reversal in the time of worship and in the time of church school, as well as a change in hours for Laurys Station.

Schedule in Effect	Proposed Schedule
Church School —9:00 A.M.	Worship Service—8:15 A.M.
Worship Service—10:00 A.M.	Church School —9:30 A.M.

Both the council and the consistory at Laurys Station expressed the feeling that their people would not agree to such a change and requested that the consultants meet with them at a later date to see if another solution could be found.

It probably would have been possible for the union church at Laurys Station to continue its ministry undisturbed by changes in the structure of its community for many years. The growth of the community did not demand that the union be broken to meet challenges as in many other communities. There were no disagreements among the members of the two congregations. The local leadership was effective. The hours for worship and church school, which they had kept for so many years, suited the schedules of their people and they were satisfied. The need for change in another congregation, however, made it necessary for the Laurys Station people to re-think their total program. Should they accede to Egypt's wishes? Should they demand that the schedules not be changed, thereby preventing the Egypt congregation from moving ahead in its program? Should they withdraw from the parish arrangement? Should they consider another alternative—often thought about, but seldom discussed—consolidation of the two congregations?

Open Inquiry

On January 2, 1963, the council and the consistory of the Laurys Station congregations met with denominational consultants to consider the alternative questions. The schedule proposed by the Egypt congregations was totally unsatisfactory to the congregations at Laurys Station. The council and consistory did not want to prevent the Egypt congregations from improving their own programs, but they did request that any change in schedule be postponed until something more satisfactory could be worked out. There was no desire on the part of the local congregations to withdraw from the parish arrangement, since neither congregation alone could support a pastor and program.

These decisions left two alternatives for the Laurys Station congregations to consider.

1. A request could be made that a new schedule, which would not affect the Laurys Station congregations so drastically, be proposed.
2. The two congregations at Laurys Station could become one and call their own pastor.

The council and the consistory reported that they had had informal discussion meetings on the possibility of having one congregation at Laurys Station. They had even made a list of the advantages to the church and community of such a consolidation. The list was presented for open discussion.

1. A consolidation would benefit the majority of the people in the community.
2. It would eliminate competition for newcomers in the community.
3. It would enhance the full program of the church.
4. It would give more guidance to the young people of the community.
5. The trend of the churches on the national level is toward consolidation and it is felt that consolidation would work on a local level.
6. The two congregations have a harmonious relationship, which would be needed in any consolidation.
7. The consensus among the members of the council and the consistory was for cooperation no matter which denomination would result.
8. The church school program could improve.
9. Worship services could be held every Sunday at a regular hour.

The consultants explained the procedures involved in the type of consolidation that was proposed. The council and the consistory was reminded that this would not be an easy adjustment, for it would necessitate one congregation's taking a vote to dissolve for the purpose of allowing the members to unite with the other. Although each member would be free to remain with the consolidated church or unite with another congregation, it would be difficult for the members to vote out of existence their congregation as a denominational unit.

It was evident that the council and the consistory had not considered this alternative lightly, for they insisted that it be discussed further in the hope of arriving at a recommendation which could be presented to the congregations. The consultants suggested that it would be advantageous to an early proposal if a group smaller in number than the council and the consistory would work on the details. It was suggested that the council and the consistory each appoint three representatives, plus one alternate, to meet with the consultants to discuss the future of the union relationship. The consultants promised that accurate minutes of the committee meetings would be kept and mailed to each member of the council and the consistory so that they might be kept informed on the procedures. A rule of anonymity would be followed in recording the procedures of the committee, which meant that no name would be listed in the minutes. By omitting names of individuals, the council and the consistory would not be influenced in reaching decisions in the knowledge that a representative of a particular congregation made a recommendation.

The inevitable question of when to go to the congregations with information on the discussions was raised. The consultants suggested that until an actual proposal had been approved by the council and the consistory, the congregations be informed only that the union relationship was under discussion. This was not intended to keep information from the congregations, but to wait until a firm proposal could be made to them. At the time of such a proposal every opportunity would be given for the people to discuss it at open meetings. Information about a consolidation without the opportunity for discussion would create some insecurity for the members and result in preconceived opinions to such an adjustment. Voting on such an important issue should be by intelligent ballot, not by uninformed opinions.

A few weeks after the initial meeting with the council and

the consistory, a study committee of three representatives of each congregation met with the consultants to consider further the question on consolidation. No thought of other types of adjustment was expressed at this time.

The size of the congregations was reported as follows:

> United Church of Christ—158 communing members
> Lutheran   — 73 communing members

Other information shared with the consultants showed equal ownership in the cemetery, church, and furnishings. All expenses for care and maintenance of the property was shared on a fifty-fifty basis.

Procedures of voting were discussed. The study committee recognized that its members would have the responsibility of making all recommendations on the matter of consolidation, including which congregation would remain and which would dissolve. The council and the consistory—as the official boards of these two congregations—would have to approve all recommendations before the congregations considered them. An attorney would be needed to word the resolution on which the congregations would vote. The congregation that would remain would vote on the question of becoming one church and would also vote on extending an invitation to the members of the other congregation to unite with them.

At this meeting the committee recommended an attorney to represent both congregations when legal advice was needed.

The second meeting of the study committee was conducted on March 11, 1963, and a favorable report was given regarding the attorney. Both the council and the consistory approved the attorney; they further agreed to pay any attorney fees on a fifty-fifty basis.

The committee stated that the council and the consistory had conducted another "unofficial" meeting and reported that there had been no change in the people's attitude that one congregation would be the answer to the Laurys Station situation. Refined reasons given for this idea were stressed as follows:

1. By having one congregation, the congregation could have its own pastor and program.
2. One congregation with one program could better serve the area and interest new people.

3. One congregation with one program could strengthen the service to the youth of the area.
4. The leadership program could be strengthened.

Consideration was given to the next step in the process— that of recommending that the churches be consolidated and deciding which congregation would remain. Much to the surprise of the consultants, the committee reported that this too had been discussed in the "unofficial" meeting of the council and the consistory and that they were prepared to make such a recommendation. In view of the larger membership of the United Church of Christ congregation, and taking into consideration the possible loss of a few members regardless of which way the decision would go, the committee unanimously felt that the resultant congregation should be United Church of Christ and that the Lutheran congregation should vote to disband.

It was suggested that discussion meetings in both congregations be held before any vote be taken. Each member would be given the opportunity to ask any question and to make any statement regarding his personal feeling in the matter. Separate meetings should be called for the purpose of voting, if the reactions in the discussion meetings were favorable.

The committee unanimously agreed to recommend to council and consistory that the Lutheran congregation vote to dissolve. The consistory of the United Church of Christ congregation would have no legal voice in this part of the recommendation, since it was a decision that would have to be made by the Lutheran council and ultimately by the Lutheran congregation. If the recommendation would be approved by the Lutheran congregation it would mean that the members of the Lutheran congregation would be free either to unite with the United Church of Christ congregation or, if they preferred to remain in the Lutheran denomination, to unite with a Lutheran congregation in another community.

Deciding the Issue

The study committee met again on April 17, and happily reported that the recommendations of the previous meeting had been approved by both the council and the consistory. The first step toward congregational action had been taken; plans were made to proceed as quickly as possible to have the congregations vote.

Two meetings were planned for the Lutheran congregation. The first meeting, for the sole purpose of discussing the recommendation, was scheduled for May 12, 1963. The consultant for the Lutheran denomination agreed to be present to answer any questions that might arise. The second meeting, scheduled for May 26, 1963, would be for the purpose of voting on the question of dissolution.

One meeting was planned for the United Church of Christ congregation for May 5, 1963, to discuss and vote on effecting one congregation and extending an invitation to the members of the Lutheran congregation to unite with them. The United Church of Christ consultant agreed to attend this meeting to answer questions.

It was now time to inform the membership officially that a recommendation concerning their future—one on which they would have the opportunity to vote—had been approved by their respective council and consistory. The consultants stressed the importance of having both congregations receive the same information on the proposal. Since the entire community would be affected by the proposed change they should share the same information so they could discuss the matter intelligently among themselves. The actual recommendation should be stated in the communication and as many reasons as possible should be included. The study committee recognized these necessities and drafted a joint letter explaining these details to be sent to the members of both congregations.

At the request of the local committee a special meeting was called on April 19, in order to clarify two important points before the congregations met to discuss the recommendations. A primary concern was to have the consolidated congregation in a position to call its own pastor. In order to do this the parish relationship with Egypt and Cementon would have to be broken. The committee agreed that the United Church of Christ congregation would vote on a request to the Conference that St. John's Church of Laurys Station be constituted a single-church charge. Implementing this vote would depend on a satisfactory vote for consolidation by the Lutheran congregation.

Another important question the committee had to face was the role of the Lutheran council in the consolidated congregation. Would any of these leaders be permitted to serve on the United Church of Christ consistory or would their official duties be ended if the Lutheran congregation voted to disband? Without hesitation the committee agreed that the Lutheran councilmen who unite with the consolidated congregation would be permitted to serve on the United Church of Christ consistory until their terms of office expired or a new constitution could be adopted by the church. The assurance was given that the United Church of Christ congregation would consider the resultant church consolidation as a *new* beginning of a *new* congregation.

When the letters to the members of the congregations in the St. John's Union Church were received, the main topic of conversation in Laurys Station was the proposed consolidation. In every home and at every gathering of people the resolution was discussed. Some of those who heard the news for the first time were strongly opposed to any change taking place in the union relationship. The union had operated satisfactorily since 1872 and, in their estimation, could continue without this kind of adjustment, which would mean the loss of identity for the Lutheran congregation. Some of the Lutheran members believed that it would be morally wrong for them even to speak in behalf of a proposed consolidation with a congregation of another denomination. There were others, however, who believed that one church could serve the community better than the two had done in the past and these people expressed favorable attitudes to the proposal. The days before the congregations met were filled with talk and speculation.

After the congregational meetings the joint council and consistory came together to think again about the future of the union church. The members had cast their votes in separate congregational meetings and no one on either the council or the consistory seemed happy about the results.

The members of the United Church of Christ consistory reported on the action of their congregation on May 5, 1963:

	Yes	*No*	*Abstaining*
To have one congregation	45	2	2
To invite the Lutheran members to unite with the United Church of Christ congregation	49	0	0
To request that St. John's be a single-church charge	49	0	0

The Lutheran council reported that its congregation had *rejected* the recommendation for consolidation by voting not to disband. The meeting, conducted on May 26, 1963, recorded the vote: Yes 22—No 36.

In the discussion that followed, the Lutheran council interpreted the action of the Lutheran congregation as being the result of (a) a number of older people who did not want to see any change, and (b) insufficient information on the recommendation before the congregation was asked to vote. The council expressed the belief that when a congregation is asked to vote on dissolution, more time should be taken to explain adequately the advantages of doing so.

Since the desire for consolidation of the two congregations had not been achieved, the council and the consistory turned again to the matter of schedule changes in the hope of helping the Egypt congregations to solve their problems. The council and the consistory at Egypt had worked on a new proposal that would enable the two congregations there to have services each Sunday and two denominational church schools and that would require a schedule change only by the Lutheran congregation at Laurys Station. This change would move the hour of worship from 10:00 A.M. to 8:15 A.M. No change would be required in the United Church of Christ schedule.

The Laurys Station council and consistory faced several alternative courses of action as they considered this new suggestion from the Egypt congregation:

1. Ask the Egypt congregations to go on an alternating schedule of worship services.
2. Ask the Egypt congregations to seek separation of the parishes and call their own pastors, thereby making it possible for the Cementon and Laurys Station congregations to create two church parishes, both of which would remain union.
3. Ask the United Church of Christ congregation at Laurys Station to vote to dissolve for the purpose of allowing the members to unite with the Lutheran congregation.
4. Accept Egypt's proposal.

The Lutheran representatives agreed to recommend that the Lutheran congregation change the hour of worship to 8:15 A.M. The Lutheran consultant agreed to meet with the council on June 11, 1963, to discuss the matter.

The Lutheran consultant, while on vacation, died on July 30, 1963. His death was a great loss to the union-church program in eastern Pennsylvania. Interim consultants were assigned by the Eastern Pennsylvania Synod of the Lutheran Church in America to work until January 1, 1964, when a new consultant would assume responsibilities.

Determination and Success

Internal difficulties in the Egypt congregations in arriving at a satisfactory decision regarding Sunday services made it impossible to put into effect the latest proposed schedule change to which the Laurys Station Lutheran congregation had agreed.

The council and the consistory at Laurys Station invited the consultants to meet with them on December 26, 1963, to reconsider the question of consolidation. The council and the consistory still maintained that one church at Laurys Station would be the answer to their problems and they wanted to discuss it further.

Since the new Lutheran consultant would not assume his duties until after the first of the year, the council and the consistory agreed to wait until then to reopen the negotiations.

On January 21, 1964, the consultants met with the joint council and consistory to review the union-church relationship. Nothing seemed settled in the community in regard to the church situation. The proposed schedule changes had not taken place and the uncertainty of what the Egypt congregations might do was cause for concern among the members. Since the people had had time to think more seriously about the vote on consolidation, it was thought that another opportunity to vote might be welcomed. A poll of the council and the consistory indicated that a majority of them still held the opinion that one church would be the best solution for this community. The council and the consistory agreed that the Lutheran congregation should vote again on the question of dissolution.

The responsibility for the planning of a satisfactory recommendation and procedure for presenting the matter to the congregations was again assigned to the study committee.

When the study committee met on March 17, 1964, the three representatives of the Lutheran congregation reported that the Lutheran councilmen who were present at the last meeting of that organization had voted unanimously to ask the Lutheran congregation to vote again on the question of dissolving for the purpose of allowing the members to unite with the United Church of Christ congregation. Such a vote by the official board of the Lutheran congregation left only the details of the voting procedure for the study committee to determine.

The committee took into consideration the observation that was made after the last vote, which indicated that the congregation had not been well-informed before it was asked to vote on dissolution. To insure that this would not be the case when the congregation would vote again, three information meetings were planned. The first and third information meetings would be for the Lutheran congregation alone, but the second information meeting would be for both congregations. A fourth meeting (for the Lutheran congregation only) would be for voting on the recommendation. The following schedule of meetings was recommended:

> June 21, 1964—A Lutheran congregational meeting to discuss the question with the Lutheran consultant.
> July 19, 1964—A joint meeting of the two congregations for the purpose of hearing a presentation on the United Church of Christ by a seminary professor, and for discussion.
> September 13, 1964—A Lutheran congregational discussion meeting with the consultant.
> September 27, 1964—The Lutheran congregational meeting to vote on dissolution.

It was agreed that a joint letter explaining these meetings should be sent to the members of both congregations.

In order to answer questions on the possible cost of having one church with a full-time pastor, the committee began to work on a proposed budget. The expense of maintaining the property would be no more than it had been in the past. Since this had always been a joint expense, a consolidation of the two congregations would not seriously affect this part of the budget. Each congregation had been paying only a portion of the salary of its pastor; however, if the consolidation would take place the responsibility for the salary of a full-time pastor would be that of the resultant congregation. It was estimated that the minimum budget for ministerial leadership would be $7,500, including fringe benefits and parsonage. Although this would necessitate a higher per capita giving responsibility of the members, it was not a discouraging matter. The members had contributed to the support of their respective congregations on a biweekly basis in the past. In a consolidation the contributions should be larger, since the one congregation would be meeting every Sunday and the members would feel the responsibility to give on a weekly basis.

The joint councils and consistories of the three union churches—Egypt, Cementon, and Laurys Station—were called together on May 6, 1964, to consider another schedule change proposed by the Egypt congregations. The new schedule would mean a change of fifteen minutes in the time of the church school and worship services at Laurys Station. It would mean a reversal of the church school hour and worship hour at the Cementon Union Church.

The members of the official boards agreed that the matter of schedule changes should be settled; it was decided that a letter would be sent to all members of the union churches at Laurys Station and Cementon, with a form at the bottom of each letter for members who were opposed to the schedule change to fill in and return to their respective council and consistory.

The Laurys Station representatives agreed to proceed with their own plans for consolidation regardless of the new proposed schedule changes.

No meetings of the study committee were conducted until after the three informational meetings of the congregations and the final voting meeting of the Lutheran congregation. When the committee met again on October 9, 1964, there were no signs of disappointment; rather there was a note of accomplishment. The Lutheran congregation had voted on September 27, 1964, to dissolve for the purpose of allowing the members to unite with the United Church of Christ congregation. Although the recommendation had been accepted by a narrow majority (Yes 28—No 24), the study committee expressed confidence that a substantial majority of the Lutheran congregation would remain with the consolidated congregation. The report was given that the congregational meetings had been friendly and interesting.

The next task of the study committee was to agree on the procedure for effecting one congregation. There were several dates to choose and a program of visiting the members of the Lutheran congregation to arrange. The Lutheran members would be visited first by the United Church of Christ pastor and representatives of the Lutheran council to determine how many would become members of the consolidated church. The Lutheran pastor would then visit those members who were undecided or who definitely wanted to remain with the Lutheran denomination. The following procedure was outlined:

1. The selection of a date when the dissolution of the Lutheran congregation would become effective.
2. The selection of a date when both pastors would resign.
3. The setting up of a visitation program of the members of the Lutheran congregation
   a) by the United Church of Christ pastor and members of the Lutheran council; and
   b) by the Lutheran pastor.
4. The legal counselor of the Eastern Pennsylvania Synod of the Lutheran Church in America would be asked to prepare documents for the purpose of transferring the Lutheran share of the property to the United Church of Christ congregation.

The representatives of the United Church of Christ congregation stated that their members had agreed in the last congregational meeting to become a new congregation if the Lutheran vote was favorable to the consolidation. To the congregation this meant that the members would be willing to have a new constitution prepared, to elect an entirely new official board with members of both former congregations eligible for election, and to select a new name for the congregation.

Another joint letter to be sent to all members of both congregations was prepared. On November 29 the Lutheran members would be received into membership of the United Church of Christ congregation, and the following committees would be appointed.

1. Pastoral placement
2. Constitution
3. Parsonage
4. Budget
5. Name of congregation
6. Nominating

The pastors agreed to resign, effective December 31, 1964. The newly consolidated congregation would begin operation on January 3, 1965. All jointly owned funds, as well as funds belonging to the Lutheran congregation, would be turned over to the newly consolidated congregation as of January 1, 1965, after all benevolences of the Lutheran congregation had been paid to the Lutheran Synod. It was further agreed that an organizational meeting of the new congregation would be held on January 3, 1965.

The membership meeting of the congregation was conducted at 7 P.M. on November 29, 1964. Both consultants who had worked in the negotiations shared in the evening sermon. Seventy-one members of the Lutheran congregation joined with the United Church of Christ congregation by letter of transfer. Four others were received by reaffirmation of faith, and the members of the United Church of Christ congregation renewed their own vows. Committees were appointed to bring into being on January 3, 1965, a fully organized *new* United Church of Christ congregation. The officers of the Penn Northeast Conference of the United Church of Christ affirmed the congregation as a single-church charge, effective January 1, 1965.

The negotiations for consolidation were brought to a close. The congregation met at 1:30 P.M. on January 3, 1965, and voted on the name of St. John's United Church of Christ, Laurys Station, Pennsylvania. A new constitution was adopted and a new consistory with representation of former Lutheran councilmen was elected. (A former Lutheran member was elected chairman of this consistory.) A budget was adopted and property from the Lutheran congregation was received. The Penn Northeast Conference and the United Church Board for Homeland Ministries agreed to aid the congregation financially in the amount of $2,500 the first year.

The first full-time pastor of St. John's United Church of Christ, Laurys Station, was elected on January 17, 1965. He began his ministry on February 1, 1965. The congregation agreed to purchase a house in the community to be used as a parsonage.

The consolidation had taken place without the difficulties many had expected. The 233 members of the new congregation represented active and unquestionable proof that ecumenicity can be achieved in a local congregation where there is a serious desire to move forward in understanding love. Many would undoubtedly think that this kind of adjustment would be less difficult in a union church than in a community where two or more buildings house separate congregations. This is not true. It was just as difficult for the Lutheran members to give up their Lutheran affiliation as it is for any other congregation. Others may believe that there is less difficulty in settling property matters when union congregations consolidate than it is when there are two or more buildings. It is true that in a union church only one property is involved, but this is owned jointly by the two separate and distinct congregations belonging to separate denominations. The mechanics of the transfer of ownership of property that have been worked out for union congregations works just as well when several buildings are involved. If consolidation is the best solution for the spiritual welfare of a community, then the details of accomplishing it, including the transfer of property, can be worked out. The people of Laurys Station, Pennsylvania, have proven it.

B
St. Paul's (Smoke) Lutheran Church (L.C.A.)
R. D., Hamburg, Pennsylvania

The Pennsylvania German people frequently refer to their churches by colloquial names rather than by the formal, official names their ancestors chose. In many communities the colloquial name is so much a part of the congregation that many have forgotten the existence of any other name. On the outskirts of Hamburg, Pennsylvania, the St. Paul's Union Church has been referred to as "Smoke Church" longer than anyone can remember. Some believe that this name originated because the updraft of the chimney was ineffectual. This caused the furnace to pour forth billows of smoke, which seeped into the sanctuary to greet the worshipers on Sunday morning. Others have said that a minor fire once caused one wall to be blackened by smoke and since it was not possible to repaint the wall immediately, this became a prominent identification of the church. There may be other explanations, but whatever may be the origin of the nickname, when a person refers to "Smoke Church" around Hamburg, everyone knows exactly which church is meant.

When St. Paul's Union Church was organized in 1756, Hamburg Borough was the trade center for the farmers in that area. There were both Lutheran and Reformed (later United Church of Christ) congregations in Hamburg at this time, but the people who lived on farms to the east of the borough wanted a church of their own nearer their homes. A plot of land was donated for the construction of a colonial, stone building approximately three miles east of the borough. When the building was completed the two congregations (Lutheran —United Church of Christ) began to use the facilities on much the same basis as described in the case study of the Laurys Station Union Church.

Between 1950 and 1960 the population of Hamburg Borough decreased by 58 persons to a total of 3,747. During the same decade, the population of the county (Berks) had increased by 20,000. Most of the county increase, however, had taken place in the city of Reading, approximately 16 miles south of Hamburg.

Due to the excellent highway systems adjacent to the Hamburg area, it is expected that this borough will one day be a highly industrialized center and that the pattern of residential housing will be drastically altered. A watershed project is scheduled for the area and is expected to be completed in about ten years. If the present projections are correct, this project will inundate several homes and two church buildings.

St. Paul's Union Church, although outside the watershed project area, will be affected by it due to the changes it will cause elsewhere. The members of St. Paul's have already had their lives altered by the industrial revolution and the decline of farming as a basic source of income for the area. The members of the church are mostly skilled or semiskilled workers who are employed in Hamburg, Allentown, Reading, and elsewhere.

There was no spectacular growth in the area around St. Paul's Church, as the members in 1756 might have expected. The two congregations never grew in terms of membership, which would have enabled either of them to support its own pastor and program. Through the years several parish arrangements were necessary to assure ministerial leadership for both congregations in their separate worship programs. In 1964 the Lutheran congregation was in a parish arrangement with one other congregation, and the United Church of Christ (UCC) congregation shared a pastor with two other congregations. At that time the membership of the Lutheran congregation was 150 and the UCC membership was 74.

The church school program, which was union from the

beginning of its organization, had some growth through the interest and participation of nearly all the members of both congregations. In 1964 the church school enrollment was 192. The church building was designed primarily for a preaching ministry; there were no facilities for an adequate Christian education ministry. The basement was partially excavated some years ago to accommodate one class of children. The largest available space for classroom study was the church sanctuary, which had no dividing partitions. Even though classes were structured according to the age of students, they could be separated only by a few rows of pews. Sight and sound made concentration on the lesson being taught by individual teachers almost impossible.

For some time the two congregations had contemplated building an addition to the church to provide space for an improved Christian education program. One of the suggested procedures of the Commission on the Welfare of the Union Church is that its consultants be invited to discuss the union relationship before any building program is undertaken. Thus the council and the consistory extended an invitation to the consultants in the hope that satisfactory arrangements could be made for early construction of these new facilities.

The First Step

The first meeting between the council, the consistory, and the consultants took place on January 2, 1964. Those who had worked on the plans for the new building indicated some disagreement as to where the building should be located. Some wanted the new structure to extend behind the existing church buildings so that the architecture of the old building would not be marred. To accomplish this, a house that was owned by the church and used as the sexton's home would have to be moved. Others wanted the new construction to be attached to the east side of the older building.

During the discussion that followed, the consultants cautioned the council and the consistory to consider all the alternatives open to the congregations before beginning any new construction. These alternatives were listed and discussed.

1. The congregations could remain in the union relationship without constructing new facilities. The overcrowding condition of the church school program would remain.

2. The congregations could remain in the union relationship and construct the new addition.
3. The joint use of facilities could continue on a shared basis. The union church school could be dissolved, and separate denominational church schools could be organized. By rearranging the schedules, this would immediately increase the available space without cost to either congregation.
4. The union relationship could be dissolved. This could be achieved in one of several ways:
   a) One congregation could sell its equity to the other, move out, and build another church.
   b) One congregation could sell its equity to the other and merge with another congregation of the same denomination in the area.
   c) One congregation could disband. The members could unite with any church of their own denomination. There would be no equity payments.
   d) One congregation could vote to dissolve for the purpose of allowing the members to unite with the other and effect a consolidation. There would be no equity payments. Each member would be free to transfer his membership wherever he chose.

Members of the council and the consistory indicated that there were questions in their own minds on what the future of the union-church relationship might be in the face of a declining population in the area.

The consultants suggested that a committee of three from each congregation be appointed to consider in more detail all the alternatives open to the congregations. The council and the consistory agreed that this would be the best procedure.

The appointed six-member study committee and the consultants met on February 13, 1964, and proceeded to discuss the alternatives as outlined above. Alternatives 1 and 3 were eliminated immediately as inadequate solutions to the particular problems faced by the congregations. Discussion on alternative 2 raised some questions concerning the ability of each congregation separately to meet half of the cost of any new construction. Preliminary estimates on the construction costs were set at $30,000. Members of the UCC congregation expressed concern as to the ability of their membership to assume obligation for half of this amount.

The possibility of dissolving the union relationship in order to effect a consolidation of the two congregations (alternative 4-d) was seriously considered. The committee agreed that even though a consolidation would take place, a new addition for Christian education would still be needed. It was pointed out, however, that the resultant congregation could undertake a realistic building program to meet the needs that would exist after the transfer of members had taken place. This congregation would be responsible for the full cost of the construction, thus eliminating the need for a cumbersome arrangement and the unequal sharing of costs on a two-congregation basis.

When the committee met again on April 16, 1964, the question of the most effective ministry needed in the area was first on the agenda. Although there seemed to be some opposition to the idea of consolidation—as was reported from the discussions in the council and the consistory meetings that had followed the last meeting of the study committee—the hope was expressed that it might be accomplished. The committee shared the belief that one congregation, with a service of worship and a church-school program every Sunday at a regular hour, would have a stronger influence on the total community.

The action necessary to effect one congregation was noted:

1. A recommendation that one congregation vote to dissolve for the purpose of consolidating with the other would be made to the council and the consistory. In consideration of the difference in the size of the congregations (Lutheran—150; UCC—74) the UCC congregation probably should be the one to vote to dissolve.
2. If the consistory would agree to the recommendation, it could be presented to the congregation for discussion and later for vote. An affirmative vote to dissolve would mean that each member would be able to choose the church he wanted to belong to, but it would be assumed that most of the active members would stay at St. Paul's and become Lutheran.
3. The Lutheran congregation could vote to extend an invitation to the UCC members to unite with it.
4. No equity would be paid if this kind of adjustment were effected.

The committee was cautioned that the motive for becoming one congregation should be on a higher basis than economics. The improved ministry to the area should be the primary consideration, the one to be emphasized in any forthcoming discussions.

The advantages of having one church were listed:

1. Church services every Sunday at a regular hour.
2. One minister to direct one program for all the people.
3. One set of leaders.
4. One inclusive program.
5. Standardized church school program.
6. Improvement in stewardship.
7. A single witness to the community.
8. More inclination on the part of the people of the community to unite with the church as a result of one program and one ministry.

The only disadvantage mentioned was the strong denominational ties of the members.

A Proposal Is Made

When the study committee completed its list of advantages, its members made a unanimous recommendation to the council and the consistory that the union relationship be dissolved and that the United Church of Christ congregation vote to disband for the purpose of effecting one congregation which would be affiliated with the Lutheran Church in America. Since the UCC congregation would be affected more seriously by this recommendation, the UCC consultant agreed to meet with the consistory when the recommendation was discussed.

The consistory considered the recommendation on April 29, 1964, in an honest effort to determine the best course of action for the UCC congregation. There was some opposition to the congregation's voting itself out of existence after more than one hundred years of denominational witness in the community. Some believed that a consolidation of the two congregations would not solve the problems of the church. Others, however, were quick to accept the advantages as listed by the study committee and examined the whole issue in terms of an expanded ministry. It was agreed that the congregation should be given an opportunity to discuss the proposal and, if no serious opposition was raised, to vote on the question of dissolution for the purpose of consolidating into a single Lutheran congregation.

A letter was drafted to be mailed to all members of the UCC

congregation to inform them of the recommendation and the date of the discussion meeting.

A specially called meeting of the UCC congregation was held on October 11, 1964, to discuss the recommendation. Serious consideration was given by all the members to the full meaning of such a recommendation for the total ministry in the area. Although some members indicated they would like to retain their membership in the United Church of Christ—and probably would not unite with the consolidated church—it was agreed that the congregation should vote on the question.

A Decision Is Made

On October 25, 1964, the UCC congregation gathered in the sanctuary of the church to take such a vote. Those who had been opposed to consolidation did not raise a strong protest at this time. Each member considered his vote in accordance with his understanding of the church's mission and the most effective way in which that mission could be performed. When the ballots were counted, 23 members believed that one congregation was the answer; 17 members wanted no change. The vote opened the way for consolidation. The Lutheran congregation had already extended an invitation to the UCC members to unite with it if the vote was favorable.

When the council and the consistory met on November 4, 1964, they took immediate steps to implement the action of the two congregations to unite themselves. The procedure to be followed was outlined.

1. Set the date when dissolution of the UCC congregation would become effective.
2. Set the date of resignation of the UCC pastor. (There was no Lutheran pastor at the time.)
3. Set the date when the consolidation into one Lutheran congregation would become effective. Plan a visitation program of the families of the UCC congregation by members of the Lutheran council.
4. Ask the UCC pastor to prepare letters of transfer for his church's members who decide to join the Lutheran congregation.
5. Have the UCC pastor visit the undecided members of the UCC congregation and issue letters of transfer to other congregations if requested. The church records of those who wanted to wait longer for a decision would be held by the UCC Conference for at least one year.

It was agreed that any UCC consistoryman who chose to unite with the Lutheran congregation would be allowed to serve on the Lutheran council until the expiration of his term of office or the adoption of a new constitution.

The council and the consistory agreed that all UCC members would be visited by December 1, 1964. This would make it possible to start the new year as a single Lutheran congregation. The last service for the UCC congregation would be conducted on December 20, 1964. The UCC pastor would submit his resignation effective January 1, 1965, which was also to be the effective date of the dissolution of the congregation. A special service of organization of the new Lutheran congregation was planned for January 3, 1965.

The service to organize the consolidated St. Paul's Lutheran congregation was inspirational. The Lutheran consultant served as liturgist for the service and the UCC consultant brought the message. At the appropriate time in the service the names of 33 former members of the UCC congregation were read by their former pastor. These members were received into the Lutheran congregation by letters of transfer. The members of the Lutheran congregation stood as a group to renew their own church vows and welcome the new members into their midst.

At the time of this study, only 15 UCC members had united with other UCC congregations in the area. The remaining 26 were undecided about their future membership, but were attending services at St. Paul's Lutheran Church; it was expected that they would eventually join this congregation.

The unity achieved in this consolidation has exceeded the people's expectations. The church is making a responsible approach in its mission to the community, and its regular schedule and improved conditions are attracting other people. Plans are now underway for the construction of the new addition. It can now be built without confusion.

Chapter Seven

✛

St. Paul's Evangelical United Brethren Church West Valley, New York

FORTY-THREE MILES southeast of the metropolitan area of Buffalo, New York, in a predominantly rural area of dairy farming, the village of West Valley is slowly adapting itself to a changing society. This change is evident in the dozen or more new homes, which have been built in the past few years, and in the towering structure of a nuclear service plant recently constructed on a site just three miles north of the village. The unpainted, tumbling structure of the general store contrasts sharply with the newness and modern design of the latest home in the village. There are no modern gas stations or supermarkets in West Valley. The past did not demand such up-to-date services, and the lone service station, the general store, and the variety shop provided all that was necessary to meet the demands placed upon them by a contented people. The nearest town of any size is Springville, about ten miles away.

Since its beginning, the village has been a stable, cloistered community. The population in 1950 was approximately 375. In 1960 the number of people had increased to 400. By 1965, with the advent of the nuclear service plant and the desire of some people to get away from the crowded conditions of the city, the population increased to 505. The local citizens expect the increase to continue as more people are employed in this one industry and as other people from Buffalo decide to move to a quieter community.

Several denominational groups have attempted to care for the religious welfare of the community at various times through the years. A Baptist congregation ministered to the community until about 1898, when it had to close because of lack of support. A Seventh-day Adventist congregation moved in and built another building for worship, but it too had to close for lack of support. St. Paul's Evangelical United Brethren Church, dating its beginning to 1869, maintained strength through the years partly because it sought to minister to the German-background people of the community in their own language. The congregation grew slowly and erected its own building on Main Street, where it is presently located. The West Valley Methodist Church traces its beginning to a segment of the Protestant community that continued services after the closing of the Baptist church. This segment became a community church, which for some years held services in the old Baptist building (now the firehall). The group later leased the Seventh-day Adventist church and purchased it when that group discontinued its work in 1922. In 1925 the building, then located on Main Street, was moved to a new location several blocks nearer the center of the village. A Roman Catholic church has continued in the village since the early days of its history. The nearest other Protestant church— a Christian Missionary Alliance congregation—is three miles distant.

Seeking a New Dimension

Early in 1963 the lay leaders of the Methodist and Evangelical United Brethren congregations began to consider the future of the church in the community in the face of the growth of the area and the ministry they had to perform. They considered the physical facilities available in the two church buildings and the duplication of program that the two congregations presented to the community. Both congregations had adequate facilities to meet their present needs, but would these facilities be adequate for the future? The Methodist congregation was in a two-point parish relationship with a Methodist congregation in Ellicottville, a community approximately eleven miles south of West Valley. The pastor lived in Ellicottville. The members of the Methodist congregation faced the question of whether or not they could meet any new growth in the area under these arrangements.

The informal discussions turned into more serious consideration as some people suggested a possible consolidation of the two congregations to improve the Protestant Christian witness in the village and surrounding area. These laymen could envision a church building being constructed to meet the needs of a larger congregation. They considered the proposed consolidation of the two denominations on a national level and asked what such a consolidation would mean to their separate units. They considered their numerical strength at the time (the Methodist congregation had 73 members and the Evangelical United Brethren congregation had 119) and the wisdom of trying to maintain separate facilities and separate programs.

When the people of West Valley began conversations on consolidating the two Protestant churches, it was not really a new idea. The thought had been implanted in the community by the New York Council of Churches some time earlier. A report on the effectiveness of the town and country churches in the state, along with suggestions for improvements, had been given by the council of churches following its study on the location, membership, and parish alignments of the congregations of all the denominations in each region of the state. From this report came the suggestion that the Methodist and Evangelical United Brethren congregations in Ellicottville be united to form a single Methodist congregation, and that the Methodist and Evangelical United Brethren congregation in West Valley be united to form a single Evangelical United Brethren congregation. The Ellicottville congregations had rejected the suggestion as impractical for them. The West Valley congregations had done nothing about the suggestion at the time it was given, but the people had not forgotten. In their own time and way, they began to move in this direction.

After the people in the community began talking, the trustees of both congregations agreed to meet together officially to consider all that might be involved in a consolidation, including what steps would be necessary to achieve this goal. The district superintendents of both communions were notified of this decision. The superintendents made no objections to the conversations, and the people were encouraged to proceed.

It should be noted that the trustees had no outside leadership to meet with them in their first series of meetings. Without the leadership of someone experienced in this type of negotiation the trustees faced a difficult question: Where should they begin in the discussions? Should they start with mission, or program, or ministerial leadership, or finances, or building? The first of the series of meetings took place on May 29, 1963, and it seemed most logical to these people that the question of building should be settled first. For the trustees at least, the idea of consolidation seemed to hinge on their vacating both existing church buildings and erecting a new building to house the combined congregation.

By starting at this point, it was necessary for the trustees to acquire sufficient information to answer the questions that the members would undoubtedly ask. They would have to know the size of building that would be needed, what kind of structure it would be, how much it would cost, and how the cost could be financed. The trustees felt that the simplest and quickest way of obtaining this information would be to make several pilgrimages to recently constructed church buildings in the surrounding area and ask their questions of others who had experience in these matters. Plans for the tour of churches were made on June 28, 1963, and an itinerary was drawn up. The first visitations were scheduled to begin the following Sunday afternoon, June 30.

The Methodist pastor reported that he had informed the Methodist congregation in Ellicottville of the discussions that were taking place in West Valley. The sharing of information with the Ellicottville Methodist Church was considered essential, due to their parish relationship. Up to this point there had been no official communication to the members of the two congregations in West Valley. The informal discussions, which had preceded the first meeting of the trustees, were considered sufficient announcement that a change in the church relationship was under consideration.

Twelve persons took part in the tour of several newly constructed church buildings on June 30. Not enough information was obtained to enable the trustees to make a recommendation on a building program; however, the visits did lead them toward a new approach on the matter of consolidation. When the trustees met with the two pastors on September 25, 1963, they agreed to go to the members of both congregations with a questionnaire, which they hoped would reveal the interest of the people in having the two congregations unite. The two pastors and one member from each congregation were given the task of formulating a questionnaire, which was to be ready for distribution by early October, 1963.

Discovering the Will of the People

The trustees, with the help of the pastors, drafted a letter that gave some background on the beginning of the negotiations. The letter, along with the questionnaire, was mailed to every home of the entire membership. The members were requested to complete the questionnaire and to return it to the trustees by November 4, 1963.

The following questions were included on the form:

1. Are you prepared to seek God's will in this matter (consolidation) through prayer and meditation?   Yes___No___
2. Do you feel that the spiritual life of the West Valley community would be improved by a consolidation of the Methodist and Evangelical United Brethren churches here?   Yes___No___
3. Do you favor further attempts to find a satisfactory basis for consolidation of the two churches, calling in the district superintendents of both denominations and others who might give counsel in the procedure for such union?   Yes___No___
4. Would you support such a consolidation if passed through official congregational channels of both churches?   Yes___No___
5. Do you oppose such attempts and feel that further discussions should be dropped entirely?   Yes___No___

Eighty-seven letters with questionnaires had been sent to the members of the Evangelical United Brethren church and 69 completed forms were returned. Sixty-seven members gave an affirmative answer to the first four questions. The trustees classified the remaining two opinions as "neutral."

Only 62 questionnaires had been mailed to the homes of Methodist members. Thirty-nine forms were returned, and of these, 36 reported favorable opinions on the proposed consolidation and asked that the talks move forward. Three Methodist members gave a negative response to the questions.

The number of affirmative replies was exceptional. This was a clear indication that the members of both congregations had given serious thought to a possible union. The trustees were encouraged as they proceeded with the negotiations.

The Methodist district superintendent, to whom the Methodist congregation had reported the progress being made in West Valley, died on January 12, 1964. An interim district superintendent was appointed until a new superintendent could take office later in the year.

A Vote to Proceed

The interim superintendent and the superintendent-elect met with the Methodist congregation on February 16, 1964, to review the status of the negotiations and to determine if the congregation wished to continue to work toward a union with the Evangelical United Brethren congregation. A ballot was taken and the congregation voted unanimously to proceed with the discussions. This, too, was an exceptional vote for the Methodist congregation at this stage of the negotiations. It had not yet been officially determined that the consolidated congregation would be affiliated with the Evangelical United Brethren denomination, although this was assumed by the community.

A special quarterly conference of the Methodist congregation was called on March 15, 1964, for the purpose of making a decision. The quarterly conference in the Methodist Church is the official board of the congregation, which must approve matters of this nature before the question can be put to a vote in the congregation. The new district superintendent presided at this meeting and, since the quarterly conference was conducted at a time when the entire congregation was together, agreed to convene a special congregational meeting to vote on the question if the quarterly conference agreed.

Following a lengthy discussion the quarterly conference voted on the motion that the Methodist congregation should consolidate with the Evangelical United Brethren congregation, and that the consolidation should become effective on June 1, 1964. Eight votes were cast in the affirmative and four in the negative. This made it possible for the entire congregation to vote on the same motion, so the district superintendent called the congregation to order for this purpose. Ballots were distributed to all members of voting age who were present. Results of the congregational vote were: 12 affirmative, 9 negative. Although this would normally be considered a sufficient majority to accomplish the consolidation, the district superintendent felt that the vote was too close to be decisive on such an important matter. The quarterly conference was asked to reconsider the original motion. The meeting of the congregation was recessed, but not dismissed, while the reconsideration took place.

When the quarterly conference was again in session, the discussion centered around the effective date of the consolidation. Time was needed to work out the details of a union that would be acceptable to both congregations; the members of the quarterly conference believed that at least one year should be allowed for this purpose. A ballot was taken to ask the Methodist congregation to vote on a consolidation with the Evangelical United Brethren congregation, effective June 1, 1965. The motion was approved without a dissenting vote.

The congregation was again assembled to vote on the resolution that had just been approved for its consideration. When the ballots were counted, eighteen members had declared themselves in favor of this consolidation while only three members voted against it. The majority had indicated the will of the congregation, and the vote was approved.

This action of the Methodist congregation was even more unusual in that the Evangelical United Brethren congregation was not asked to vote on any question at this time. In fact the Evangelical United Brethren congregation voted only on one question in the whole process and that was the acceptance of a plan and basis of union which the committee formulated later.

The normal procedure of voting on questions of consolidation indicates that each congregation should vote on the same questions at the same time. If the schedule of congregational meetings for such votes cannot be planned simultaneously, then they should be planned as close together in time as schedules will permit. Even when the denominational relationship for the resultant congregation is predetermined, the congregation of that affiliation should vote to extend an invitation to the members of the other congregation (s) to join with them in the creation of a new congregation of this denomination.

When only one congregation votes on a matter such as this, the impression is given that that congregation is giving up everything and the other congregation (s) is not required to make such demanding decisions. The trustees in West Valley accepted the overwhelming affirmative opinion of the Evangelical United Brethren members (determined through the questionnaire) as expressing their will for the consolidation. The difference in the size of the congregations also entered into the decision of the resultant denominational affiliation. It was felt, therefore, that the Evangelical United Brethren congregation should not vote on anything other than the conditions of the union, which were to be presented later.

The trustees were now faced with the task of bringing the two congregations together in such a way as to strengthen the total Protestant witness in the community through a more effective program. They would have to develop ways to integrate the best of both into a harmonious unit and to do it in such a way that few members would be lost in the transition. They began this mountainous task on April 13, 1964, at which time several questions regarding matters that had not been seriously discussed before faced them immediately. Some of the more important were:

1. What will be done with the present Methodist property?
2. How will the transition of membership take place?
3. How will the official board of the new congregation be decided?

Reorganization and Strengthening the Committee

In the discussion that followed, it became obvious that the trustees would need the counsel of other members of the congregations in working through all the details of the union. The trustees decided to invite the president and one member of each of the women's societies, the superintendent and one member of each church school, and the directors of each youth group to serve with them as a committee on consolidation.

The first meeting of this committee was conducted on April 29, 1964. One of its first acts was to create subcommittees with specific responsibilities for developing satisfactory agreements in their particular areas of concern for work in the new church. The subcommittees created were:

1. Church school
2. Women's work
3. Youth work
4. Property and equipment
5. Finance and budget

6. Membership and representation (the total committee would
serve in this capacity)
7. Fellowship

It was understood that each of these committees could co-opt
other members of the congregations whenever necessary.

The committees were assigned the task of studying the needs
of each organization and program as these would be affected
by the consolidation. Suggestions and recommendations were
needed to insure that every group would have a voice in the
structure of a new congregation. Each committee was asked to
meet separately to formulate its own recommendations and to
report to the total committee on consolidation within two
months.

In the midst of this critical period in the negotiations, the
pastor of the Methodist congregation was reassigned. A new
pastor was appointed to serve the congregation until the consolidation would be consummated. Although the change in
pastors did not ultimately delay the union, it did cause some
concern in the community. The new pastor had to become
acquainted with all that had taken place in the negotiations
before his arrival. This responsibility, added to the normal
adjustments required of any pastor who accepts a new field,
did result in some delay in completing the agreements on the
consolidation. It is always to the advantage of the congregations involved in negotiations of this type to maintain the
same pastoral leadership until the final decisions have been
made.

When the full committee on consolidation met on June 23,
1964, the subcommittees reported on the progress of their
work.

1. Church School—The estimated number in the church school
program after the consolidation would be 162. It was believed that two or three of the classes would be too large to
be accommodated by the existing facilities in the Evangelical
United Brethren church. Although the possible use of both
buildings had been discussed by the committee, it was felt
that the entire church school should be housed in the same
building. A further survey of the membership and facilities
was planned.
2. Women's Organization—The combined membership of the
two women's groups was estimated at 58. The subcommittee

discussed the possibility of having the women meet for program and service in small circle groups with periodic meetings
of all the women.

3. Youth Work—The subcommittee on youth work did not
   meet in the interim, since a consolidation of the youth
   program of the two congregations was already an accomplished fact.
4. Property and Equipment—It was agreed that the subcommittee on property and equipment should seek the services of an
   attorney in the matter of transfer of property.
5. Finance and Budget—The subcommittee had met to com-
   pare membership rolls and financial reports of the two congregations. It was recommended that any future plans for
   additional building should be reflected in the financial planning of the new church.
6. Fellowship—The subcommittee reported a scheduled joint
   fellowship dinner for September, 1964.

Following a discussion on membership and representation
on the official board in the new church, it was agreed that
several members of the Methodist congregation should consult
with the Methodist district superintendent on the manner in
which the transfer of members to the Evangelical United
Brethren church would be effected.

A period of six months followed, during which no action
was taken and no committee meetings were conducted. When
the committee on consolidation did meet on January 23, 1965,
the district superintendents of both congregations were present and served as cochairmen during the discussion.

The committee was asked to prepare a document that
would include all its recommendations on effecting the consolidation. This document would, in fact, be a plan and basis of
union for the two congregations. The district superintendents
outlined the work that the committee should accomplish in
preparing this document. They also requested that, when the
plan was completed, it should be shared with each of them
before the congregations would be asked to take any action.

The subcommittee that had the responsibility of studying
the needs of a consolidated church school reported that their
members agreed that the facilities of the Evangelical United
Brethren church would be adequate for the church school
program.

The Methodist pastor was instructed to write a personal
notice to each Methodist member to determine which mem-

bers would transfer to the Evangelical United Brethren congregation and which would unite elsewhere.

The sharing of joint worship services had not been a frequent practice of the two congregations. It now seemed advantageous to the consolidation effort to ask the congregations to share this experience. The first Sundays in April and May were designated for this purpose and both pastors were asked to share in these services.

The official date for the uniting service was set for June 6, 1965. The Methodist congregation would meet in its own building at 10:50 A.M. and proceed from there to the Evangelical United Brethren church where the two district superintendents would consummate the consolidation.

Plan and Basis of Union Recommendations

The plan and basis of union was drafted on February 24, 1965. The full committee on consolidation met for devotions and instructions before its members adjourned for the task of their respective subcommittee concerns. These subcommittees refined the recommendations of previous meetings, after which the entire committee convened to hear their reports. The plan and basis of union was formulated from these reports and sent to both district superintendents for their consideration. Among the more important considerations included in this plan were the following:

1. The board of trustees of the Methodist congregation shall be included totally as members of the board of trustees of the Evangelical United Brethren congregation.
2. The pastor of the Methodist congregation shall appoint five members from the board of stewards and the commission on stewardship and finance of the Methodist church to serve on the stewardship and finance committee of the Evangelical United Brethren church.
3. The property known as the "Methodist property" shall at no time be sold or transferred to any other Protestant group.
4. The two properties of the united church shall henceforth be known as the "School Street property" and the "Main Street property."
5. The board of trustees shall become responsible for the maintenance and use of all church properties and equipment.
6. The 1965 session of the Olean district conference of the

Methodist Church shall be requested to transfer the property known as the West Valley Methodist Church to the Evangelical United Brethren church for the consideration of one dollar.

7. An increase in the 1965 annual budget of the Evangelical United Brethren church from $12,303 to $13,803 shall be recommended.

8. All surplus funds of the West Valley Methodist Church at the time of the consolidation shall be transferred to the Evangelical United Brethren church building fund.

9. The expense of maintenance of the School Street property shall be assumed by the board of trustees of the Evangelical United Brethren church.

10. All money in the Methodist church school treasury at the time of consolidation shall be turned over to the Evangelical United Brethren church school treasury.

11. The Methodist church school staff shall be incorporated in the Evangelical United Brethren church school staff.

The plan and basis of union was now ready to be presented to the congregations for approval. The important questions that might be raised by the congregations were answered through the excellent work of the committee in the detail of the recommendations. The district superintendents met again with the committee on April 26, 1965, and set the date of May 2 for a special joint meeting of the congregations to consider the plan.

Goal Accomplished

The Methodist pastor reported that he had written to each of the 73 members of the Methodist congregation on the question of their willingness to be a part of the consolidation. Fifty-nine members had responded to the letter. Forty members had agreed to go into the consolidation by requesting the transference of their memberships to the Evangelical United Brethren church. Ten members had requested transfer to other Methodist churches, and 14 requested that their names be removed from the church roll. No reply had been received from 14 members.

The request to remove the 14 members from the church roll did not necessarily mean that these people were in opposition to the consolidation. Most of these members were living elsewhere and either had united with a congregation in their new community or had been delinquent in their church membership over a period of years. The majority of the active members who lived in West Valley united with the consolidated congregation.

The two congregations joined in worship on May 2, 1965. A fellowship meal followed the worship service, and this was followed by a joint congregational meeting. Both district superintendents attended these activities.

The plan and basis of union was presented to the congregations and discussed. When all the questions of the members had been answered, a vote on the plan of union was taken. The vote was unanimous in both congregations to proceed with the consolidation on the basis of that which had been discussed.

The long-awaited day arrived. The members of the Methodist congregation gathered in their own building at 10:50 A.M. on June 6, 1965, and proceeded in solemn procession to their new church home. They were met at the Evangelical United Brethren church by their friends and neighbors who extended their warm greetings, by the two pastors who had labored with them through the negotiations for this consolidation, and by the two district superintendents who had assisted and blessed this union. Forty members of the West Valley Methodist Church accepted the covenant of membership in the Evangelical United Brethren church and thereby pledged a united witness of Protestant Christians in a community with confidence in the future.

As each person present lifted his heart and voice to God in the singing of the hymn "God of Grace and God of Glory," there was no doubt in the mind of any man that the fact of unity had been achieved.

Chapter Eight

✠

Suggested Procedure for Uniting of Churches

THE ILLINOIS COUNCIL OF CHURCHES, through its Commission on Church Planning and Development, has achieved a break-through in interdenominational relations in that state in the development of the document entitled *Suggested Procedure for Uniting of Churches*.* The document itself is no small achievement; however, the commission has not stopped there. It has cooperated in many community discussions that have resulted in the consolidation across denominational lines of more than twenty congregations. In this manner the theories of this suggested procedure have been tested and proven as one way of achieving closer cooperation and greater unity among the churches in the town and country areas of that state.

The *Suggested Procedure for Uniting of Churches* is a fur-ther development of a document written in 1962 entitled *One Lord—One Mission,* which was accepted by the state execu-tives of the twelve denominations then participating in the Illinois Council of Churches as a basis of their working to-gether. The basic affirmations of this document were:

1. The church of Jesus Christ is essentially one.
2. Within the framework of this unity, the church carries out its mission through local congregations, denominational bodies,

---

* Developed by the Church Planning and Development Commission, Illinois Council of Churches. Used by permission.

and cooperating agencies of diverse backgrounds and patterns of work.

3. For the church to speak effectively to the needs of our world, the seeking and implementing of God's will must be uppermost; denominational and institutional concerns must be under the control of God's spirit and action.

The executives further agreed:

Such statements are empty words unless they can be implemented on the local level. In town and country areas where time has brought great changes, we recognize that many churches are proving ineffective in ministry to their communities. A number of these churches were started to meet conditions that no longer exist. In many communities more churches were started than can now be justified. With radical shifts in population resulting in a population decline in many places, churches are often too small to provide an adequate ministry. Many of these churches are without pastors, served by part-time pastors or by pastors not fully trained.

Since 1963 the *Suggested Procedure for Uniting of Churches* has been used in Illinois to bring together congregations in a given community in such a way that the Holy Spirit may have a chance to work among them. When any significant deviation from this procedure has been attempted, unnecessary delays and problems have resulted.

The following outlined procedure is the full detail of the successful suggestions of the Illinois Council of Churches.

Steps Leading to Unification

I. *Why Consider It?*

The really basic reasons for congregations considering what they might do together are:

A. To give a more effective witness for Jesus Christ and his kingdom locally and worldwide.
B. To express the essential oneness of our discipleship to him and our relationship to each other as brothers and sisters under God our Father.

Other benefits may come as by-products of our working together and be used as arguments for unification, but if these become the basic reasons for coming together we may be building a new relationship for the wrong reasons and on foundations of sand. Some of these by-products are survival; better stewardship of time, abilities, leadership, and assets;

more adequate pastoral leadership; better facilities and program; and saving money.

For example, it has been found that congregations should not be told that they "save money" by getting together. Although there may be some efficiency effected by the combining of resources, it is entirely possible that to do a better job it may take "more" rather than "less" money. A better motive would be, "we hope to do a better job." Also, if we consider coming together only for "survival," this eliminates many congregations who are quite self-sufficient *but who might do a much better job* by uniting their strength with another strong church to give a united witness to the community.

Although the essential message of our faith is "reconciliation," the church is often the last institution in the community still dividing the people of the community because of sentiment or denominational loyalties.

II. *Who Starts It?*
  A. Anyone can take the initial step
    1. A layman or pastor from the local community.
    2. A member of the committee responsible for strategy in one of the denominations.
    3. One of the denominational state executives.
  B. Cooperative activities that may prepare the churches for the consideration of unification are listed below:
    1. Union services, such as those at Thanksgiving, Lent, Reformation Sunday, Worldwide Communion Sunday.
    2. A community daily vacation church school.
    3. An exchange of pulpits, particularly during summer vacation periods when one minister might serve two or more congregations at a union service or in multiple services while another pastor is on vacation.
    4. Cooperative evangelism, such as a mission to inactives or a union preaching mission.
    5. United groups, such as union choirs or choruses, youth work, men's work, and women's work.
    6. Community projects of religious and/or civic nature, such as adult schools of religion.
    7. Planned appearances of denominational executives, ministers, and laymen of the different churches together at public events.

Although the above activities probably help to set a favorable climate for the consideration of uniting, unification can be considered even if little has been done together before.

III. *However*

Once the question has been raised (regardless of who starts it), the state executive of that denomination should be contacted immediately and the initiative should be passed to him. There are three crucial reasons for this:

  A. Since these discussions are a denominational as well as a local concern, the denominational executives should be involved from the very first.
  B. Since the denominational executive is not as emotionally involved in the local situation, and because of his knowledge of other situations, he is able to be particularly helpful in setting up and guiding the process and in solving the problems that may arise.
  C. Such a sharing of responsibility in opening up the concern in the local community might prove to be very helpful in making for good, continuing pastor-parish relationships regardless of the outcome.

IV. *Who Else?*

Once an executive has been notified or has taken the initiative in a particular community, he should *immediately* get in touch with the responsible executives of the other denominations involved to learn if they are interested and willing to proceed in that particular community. If they are not, the process *should stop immediately.* Real cooperative work is not ordinarily possible unless the executives involved are favorable at least to the idea of exploring the possibilities together.

V. *If The Executives Are Favorable*

A meeting should be set up with the executives and the pastors of the churches involved. The local situation should be discussed, what is happening across denominational lines in Illinois should be talked about, the executives should express their concern for the local witness and their willingness to work together toward any good solutions, and the pastors should be asked to give their feelings about going any further. If any of the pastors are hostile toward the idea then the process *should be delayed or stopped,* as any real progress in getting congregations together is rarely possible unless the pastors in the field can become excited over the possibilities.

VI. *If the Pastors Are Willing, Then*

  A. The executives through their pastors should invite the official boards of the congregations involved to a dinner meeting in a neutral place to hear the story and to discuss "how we might work together in (name of the place) to make a more effective witness for Jesus Christ, locally and around the world." This dinner should usually be held in a private room in a restaurant. (The method for meeting the cost should be agreed upon in advance by the executives involved.) Tables should be set for eight to ten people. An equal number from each church is placed at each table, the number dependent upon how many churches are involved. Two churches will have four at each table. Three churches will have three at each table. Four churches will have two at each table. Five churches will have two at each table. If one of the churches has a large official board, it would be wise for the pastors of the other church (or churches) to invite enough of their leaders to give approximately the same number of people from each church.

B. The pastors issue the invitation on behalf of the denominational executives to the official leaders of their church. The pastors should word their invitations so as to incorporate the following idea:

As a leader in our congregation you are invited to attend a dinner meeting to be held with the leaders of the (name) church at 6:30 P.M., at the (name of place), (date), and (location). The purpose of our meeting is to discuss how we as Christians in (name of community) may work together to have a more effective ministry for our Lord, locally and around the world.

C. The pastors also work out the assignments of their people to the dinner tables so that an equal number (as far as they go) from each church will be at each table. Husbands and wives should be seated at different tables to be sure each gets to talk and to be exposed to a greater number of people. Pastors and their wives sit at the head table with the executives and strategy committee members, so that each table will feel free to discuss anything they wish. Usually the head table holds its own discussion when the other tables are in discussion. The pastors also obtain laymen to lead the hymn singing and to play the piano, if one is available. They should furnish mimeographed song sheets for the following hymns, which are common to most hymnbooks and ecumenical in content:

Faith of Our Fathers
The Church's One Foundation
In Christ There Is No East or West

D. It is at this point that the denominational executives may want to contact the Church Planning and Development Commission for the help of the researcher to make a study of the local situation. This study would then be shared with the executives, pastors, and local people in meetings which will follow. This study should probably cover information such as listed below, as well as any other information the researcher may feel is pertinent to the situation.

1. Membership trends over a period of at least the past ten years.
2. Trends in financial support over a similar period.
3. An analysis of church membership in each church as to age and sex.
4. Community characteristics, such as farming, nonfarming, rural, industrial, suburban, residential.
5. Occupational classification of the memberships of the churches.
6. A description of transportation patterns.
7. Spot map showing location of present families belonging to each church. (This information could no doubt be furnished by the local pastors.)
8. Public school districts as they relate to the community structure.
9. Pastoral leadership over at least the past ten years as to length of service, ministerial status, and proportion of time given to their churches.
10. Building facilities available.

E. The dinner program is directed by the executives and usually follows the agenda listed below:

Invocation—Executive or strategy committee
Dinner
Hymn Sing—Led by a layman
Why We Are Here—Executive
1. Word of appreciation and welcome.
2. We have come to break bread together and to discuss "How we may work together in (name of community) to make a more effective witness to Christ, locally and around the world."
3. No decisions other than what our next step should be, if any, will be made here tonight.

The Local Situation—Executive

Here a mimeographed study of the local church and community statistics should be handed out and explained. If the researcher for the Illinois Council of Churches has made a study, this could be mimeographed and shared with the local people; otherwise a study will have to be prepared by one of the executives involved. This mimeographed study will then be used later as the basis for discussion of one of three questions.

The State and Worldwide Situation—Executive

The rapidly developing social revolution should be outlined. Population explosion, urbanization of society, the high living standards, the mobility of our people, the transportation revolution, technological changes should be outlined.

What is happening in Illinois? (such as population growth or decline, shift of population from rural to urban)

What are the strategic alternatives facing our churches in the town and country areas? (See study material, if available.) Graphs and other data should be shared with the group and the implications of the data outlined.

Discussion Groups

Each group around each of the dinner tables becomes a discussion group.

The person whose last name is nearest to the letter "A" becomes the chairman or discussion leader. His job is to get the others to talk.

The person whose last name is nearest to the letter "Z" becomes the secretary. His job is to record the important points of their discussion and to note any questions that his group would like to hear answered by the experts. The following questions are given out one at a time and discussed for about fifteen minutes each.

1. *What is our present situation?* (See local statistical sheet passed out earlier in the meeting.)
   What is the leadership potential?
   Are there to be choirs; other special groups?
2. *What might we do or be if we worked together in some way or ways?*
3. *Which of the alternatives listed below might work for us here?*
   a) Stay as we are.
   b) Dissolve one or more of the churches and encourage the members to go to another nearby Protestant church.
   c) Become "yoked" (share the same pastor).
   d) Become an "area" church. All churches are dis-

solved and their members are gathered into a central church, possibly in a county seat town.

e) Become members of a cooperative parish.
f) Become yoked churches, but with the hope of later uniting.
g) Unite our churches to form a united witness in the community.
h) Other.

Group Reports

These reports are made by the secretaries to the whole group at the meeting. The executives and pastors do not come to this meeting with any preconceived ideas of what should be done in this particular situation. The Holy Spirit is given free rein to lead the people where they should go, and their prayer should be that the people will follow his lead. *The only suitable answer in a given community is the one that the people will willingly and enthusiastically accept and do.* Some communities simply are not ready to go as far as we would sometimes like to see them go, so it is agreed ahead of time to honor whichever alternative seems best to them and to work with them in using it to make their church more effective.

An enthusiastic spirit and a good sense of humor are invaluable for the success of these meetings. Many an uneasy moment may be turned to good with the right touch of humor.

Some of the reports will be outstanding. Some of the statements and witnesses to our faith will be great. Some will be negative and hostile. But everyone should feel perfectly free to express his deepest feelings and to give the whole group a chance to react to them. We often see real miracles of change in attitudes and deep reconciliation because of the warm spirit of people who are struggling together to serve our Lord more effectively, despite sentiment and loyalties to denominations and the past.

Questions arising from the discussion groups give the executives the opportunity to dispel many fears and to demonstrate their commitment to cooperative work in Illinois. The spirit among the executives in Illinois has been both gratifying and inspirational. There has been real mutual respect, trust, and affection toward each other. This has often led the congregations to have the same respect, trust, and affection for each other as they sense what this means to the churches and to the kingdom, and what it could mean to them in their witness to each other and the world.

Some of the crucial questions often asked are:
1. What will happen to the local church property of the churches involved?

Answer: In every case so far, each denomination has transferred its claim on any local assets to the new united church when unification has taken place. This will be subject, of course, to the processes required by each denomination. Also the conditions of any legacies left to the church will have to be followed, particularly if the church should ever be dissolved.

2. How will the denomination of the new united church be decided?

Answer: This will be entirely up to the local congregations. However, in order to be fair to all the congregations involved, and in order that each congregation may have a chance for the new united church to be of its denomination, and to prevent the local community from getting into any controversy over what denomination the new church will be, it is recommended that the congregations ask the Church Planning and Development Commission of the Illinois Council of Churches to recommend what their new denomination affiliation should be.

If the local congregations do decide to ask the Church Planning and Development Commission to make such a recommendation, the official boards of each of the participating churches should appoint a committee of three from each church to go to the meeting at which the matter will be considered. Each of the denominations has at least one representative on this Church Planning and Development Commission. Every situation is weighed carefully and prayerfully, and there is a spirit of fairness and a high degree of competence among the members of the commission. Since this is the same commission that makes new church assignments in new communities, it is logical that they would have information and attitudes necessary to make wise decisions in the case of denominational affiliations of churches that have been united.

3. How will the first official board be formed?

Answer: It is recommended that this be done by presenting a predetermined percentage of officers from each of the participating churches for election the first year. After the first year, the officers should probably be nominated without reference to former church membership.

4. What hymnbooks will be used and to which agencies will the benevolences be sent?

Answer: As soon as the local congregations have accepted the recommendation of the Church Planning and Development Commission as to which denomination the new united church should belong, and as soon as the churches have been officially brought together according to the procedures of the denominations involved, then the hymnals of the new denomination should be used along with other materials common to that denomination. Benevolence giving of the united church would also go to the denomination with which the new group is affiliated.

5. Other questions, which the local congregations want to decide for themselves, can be placed on a ballot, so that each person has the opportunity to express his opinion on any major issues.

Prayer Circle

The group forms a large circle and those who wish to do so give a short prayer. These prayers are usually followed with the Lord's Prayer, the leader being careful to state ahead of time whether to use "trespasses" or "debts."

Adjournment

F. After the dinner meeting the executives and the pastors meet briefly to evaluate the meeting. If the reaction seems to be unfavorable (which has been seldom so far) the process *is stopped,* with a general statement of how good it was to break bread together as Christians and to discuss mutual concerns.

If the reaction is favorable, a date is immediately cleared to get the congregations together as soon as possible. This will prevent rumors that may start in the community; thus, the congregational meeting should not be put off for too long a time.

VII. *The Congregational Meeting*

All the congregations involved are invited by the pastors of their churches, using the same invitation given to the leaders of the church, to meet at a neutral place, such as the high school gym, to hear the same story and to go through the same process as the leaders did earlier. Exactly the same program is followed as the one previously held at the dinner meeting.

Discussion groups are usually set up in circles with the same number as used at the dinner meeting. Usually some of the women of the churches have coffee and cookies ready after the meeting for those who want to linger and visit.

Following this meeting the pastors and executives again evaluate and try to determine the next step. If it is apparent that there is no disposition to work together any more closely than they have in the past, again, *the discussions and any further steps are stopped,* care being taken to comment as to how wholesome it is for Christians to get together to discuss their faith and problems.

In some cases the desire of the congregations is so apparent that it is possible to go immediately to the next step. If the churches clearly are in favor of unification, then the next step would be to call official congregational meetings to vote upon unification in accordance with the legal procedures of each denomination. It is important in setting up these congregational meetings that the churches meet at exactly the same time and vote on exactly the same ballot so that there will be no misunderstanding. Usually the congregations like to vote upon three propositions:

1. Shall the (name of church) and/or the (name of church) and/or the (name of church) unite as soon as practical and no later than (date), and shall the official boards of the two churches take the legal and other necessary steps to carry out the merger, including the transfer of such properties, assets and liabilities of each church as can legally be transferred to the united church?

2. Shall the denomination of the newly formed united church be recommended by the Church Planning and Development Commission of the Illinois Council of Churches in consultation with the official boards of the two participating churches?

3. Beginning with the organization of the new united church, shall the nominating committee, officers, and board members be made up of equal representation of each of the former congregations using the three-year rotary system, and then after the first year be chosen without reference to former affiliation?

Those congregations that express interest in working together in some way, but do not seem ready for any specific steps, should give further study to the proposition. This is often done by each official board appointing a steering committee of five people to work out further educational steps and to try to bring about some kind of further cooperative action.

Many times when the local congregations find out that the denominational executives are really not pushing them toward any certain alternative, they relax and become much more ready to give serious consideration to a cooperative venture. Since there are so many communities in which such discussions are taking place, the executives need not feel any pressure to "produce" in a particular situation. Sometimes merely sowing the seeds may produce a real harvest at some time in the future—*even ten years hence!*

VIII. *Denominational Recommendation*

A. The local congregations have the right and the responsibility to decide in which way the denomination of the new united church will be determined. In some cases the denominational affiliation is so obvious that the decision may be made locally.

B. In some cases where the congregations submit the question of denominational affiliation to the Church Planning and Development Commission of the Illinois Council of Churches, the decision of the commission would be made in the form of a recommendation that the local congregations should agree to accept, subject to the action of their denominations.

If the Church Planning and Development Commission is asked to make a recommendation as to the denominational affiliation of the new united church, the official boards of each of the participating churches should appoint at least three of their members to represent them at the next meeting of the commission. When these representatives come to the meeting they should have as much information as possible; for example, when the discussions were started and how; what the attitude of the people has been; the statistics of the local situation; the vote; and any other information that they feel would be helpful to the commission in making a decision.

These representatives should not be put on the spot by being asked to state which denomination they feel the new united church should be. After the delegation has been heard they should be dismissed, while the commission meets for prayerful consideration of all factors, and the drafting of its recommendation. The decision is not given out by the commission but is usually taken by the executives involved to a joint congregational meeting in the community, and the announcement made at that time. In most cases a brand new corporation is formed, even though at least one of the former churches would obviously already be a member of the recommended denomination. Such action enables all the members of all the churches to come into the new church on the same basis. The assets of the former church corporations are transferred to the new corporation in the manner prescribed by the government of the particular denomination.

Ordinarily the pastors of the churches involved are asked to seek a call or be given assignment to some other community. This enables the new congregation to have a clear choice as to whom its pastoral leadership will be, free of personalities and existing obligations. This seldom works a hardship on the participating pastors as other churches are often quite interested in pastors who have been successful in helping to unite congregations across denominational lines. The executives of the denomination with which the new church affiliates should be especially alert in helping them to secure outstanding pastoral leadership and to make the transition to the new fellowship as quickly and as easily as possible. It is at this time that each congregation must be most diligent in consideration of the feelings of the other people of the fellowship.

IX. *Follow-up*

Since the primary purpose in the uniting of churches is to provide a more effective witness for Jesus Christ in the local community and around the world, it is important to find out if the new united church really is more effective than the former churches were separately. This means that such things as the membership, total giving, attendance at worship and Sunday church school, total benevolence giving, the number of choirs, the number of people in leadership in the new church should be at least as great as the combined totals of these same activities in the separate churches. It is hoped, of course, that the reports of the new united church will be *greater* than the combined totals of the churches separately, although numbers alone are not the most important measure of effectiveness. The denominational executives should make an evaluation as soon as the project has been in operation long enough to judge results. Such questions should be asked as:

Is the project going well?
What achievements have been made?
In what areas has the project failed?
What seems to be the reason for the successes and/or the failures?

Even though the new united church may be the primary concern of the denomination with which it has become affiliated, all other denominations and the Illinois Council of Churches have a stake in the effectiveness of the ministry of the new united church from the standpoint of the impact it makes in the local community, as well as the kind of a witness it makes to other communities that are considering taking the same step.

X. *And Finally, Brethren* . . .

It is to be emphasized that this document contains the suggested procedure for uniting of churches. These suggested steps or actions are not rigidly established, and may be implemented with some degree of flexibility as specific needs may arise. However, the procedures have been *tried and proved,* and they will apply for *most situations.* It is probable that additional experience on the part of all of us in these matters will lead to revised and/or additional suggestions for proceeding, *as indeed we must,* in this important phase of the mission that is ours in his kingdom.